Three Plays

FALSE ADMISSIONS
SUCCESSFUL STRATEGIES
LA DISPUTE

First published in 1989 by Absolute Classics, an imprint of
Absolute Press, 14 Widcombe Crescent, Bath, England

© Timberlake Wertenbaker

Series Editor: Giles Croft

Cover and text design: Ian Middleton

ISBN 0 948230 21 5

Printed in the United States of America

FALSE ADMISSIONS
SUCCESSFUL STRATEGIES
LA DISPUTE

Three plays by

Marivaux

Translated by Timberlake Wertenbaker

absolute classics

INTRODUCTION

Marivaux, it has been said, was never destined for export from France. Even the most recent edition of the Oxford Companion to the Theatre repeats the charge: "The subtlety of his dialogue makes it almost impossible to translate him adequately into English."

Why, then, a volume of three plays in English translation?

Simply, Marivaux *has* been adequately translated into English by Timberlake Wertenbaker, and considerably more than adequately. Her meeting with the texts of Marivaux has been a fortunate one for the English stage and for the much larger audiences of British radio drama. Her translations illuminate the plays in the only way that finally matters: dramatically. While remaining faithful to the original French, she has achieved an English style which is at once formal and playful, properly mannered and relaxed. Her texts work in English, and reveal Marivaux's world.

In the past few years there has been a rush of English interest in Marivaux, the fourth most popular playwright at the *Comédie-Française* after Molière, Corneille and Racine. Two theatrical events in London did much to awaken that interest. The first was a staggeringly theatrical and sensual French production of LA DISPUTE, directed by Patrice Chéreau and presented at the National Theatre of Great Britain. The second was the production of two lovingly contrasted Marivaux plays in English by the Shared Experience company, directed by Mike Alfreds and translated by Wertenbaker.

They are the three plays which have been gathered here.

Wertenbaker brings particular qualities to her translations; qualities which achieve an unusual harmony with Marivaux's own voice. French is as much her language as English, but it is in English that she writes and her major achievements in the English theatre, most notably OUR COUNTRY'S GOOD for the Royal Court, respond to the Restoration writers, especially Marivaux's contemporary, George Farquhar. Her original plays also deal in conscious play-acting in the search of genuine emotions, a beloved technique of Marivaux as well as he constantly analyses human inconstancy. Her translations manage to reconcile the manners of Marivaux to English speech, preserving, as few other translators do, the precise, almost prissy, banter while making it playable.

Indeed, it is the playing of Marivaux that has long been one of the most difficult challenges in the theatre and even in France his reputation was not always what it is now. Voltaire was chief among his detractors, but the stultified performance style of the *Comédie-Française* perpetuated a fairyweight image of the plays for centuries. (There is a particular irony in that his greatest successes were not with the *Comédie-Française* but with the rival and long defunct *Comédie-Italienne* who brought to their work the traditions of the *commedia dell'arte*.)

All that changed in 1946 with Jean-Louis Barrault's production of LES FAUSSES CONFIDENCES (given in Wertenbaker's translation as FALSE ADMISSIONS) and virtually all the major post-war directors of French theatre have had a hand in revealing the psychological insights of Marivaux's plays along with realizing theatrically the intense sexual undercurrents that had been played previously as light love intrigues.

Not only England, and speakers of English, had to wait centuries to discover Marivaux. The French did as well.

MARIVAUDAGE
There is a reason for this, and for the legend of his immunity to translation. Very early on a French wag derided Marivaux's writing with the coinage of the word *Marivaudage*, a brisk and unfriendly summary of a writing style which was as distinct in the 1720s and onwards as Harold Pinter's style in the England of the 1960s and 1970s. The difficult is that *Marivaudage* is at once as specific and meaningless as "Pinteresque". It succeeds in describing the tone of the writing to someone who has heard it, or read it, but otherwise does nothing more than indicate that a writer uses language in a very particular way.

Nonetheless, debate has gone on for centuries over the definition of *Marivaudage*. In derogation, it is seen as the subject matter as well as the linguistic style. Marivaux is clearly guilty of writing about love and love's stratagems, and his plots do not exactly abound with action despite the frequent reversals and complications. He is therefore a slight writer who indulges in eloquent discourse on the subject of love.

Ironically, his admirers take a similar view but elevate their interpretation of his style to justify the words themselves as

psychological drama, which, as with any good dramatist, they are.
However, as with Pinter, it is what the characters do with their words
that makes the drama and with Marivaux the characters play with
language. They spin out words which, having heard aloud, they call
back or restate. They listen to themselves to find out what they mean.
His language is subtle and not easy to bring into English and it is
language which commands the attention not only of the audience, but
of the actors speaking it.

Having shed their burden of tradition in France, the plays now speak
for themselves and that is the test of any translation. Wertenbaker's
versions have passed that test, with SUCCESSFUL STRATEGIES
successful on stage, FALSE ADMISSIONS successful on both stage
and the radio, and THE DISPUTE working for BBC Radio 3 where
it conveyed a political eroticism without the additional texts and
dramaturgical paraphenalia of Cheréau's production.

MARIVAUX AND THE PLAYS
Marivaux was born Pierre Carlet de Marivaux in 1716 and had the
first professional staging of his plays in 1720. In 1721 he faced
financial ruin and turned to full-time writing to earn his living.
Although his plays were performed by both the *Comédie-Française* and
the *Comédie-Italienne*, the bulk of his successful work was with the
Italians where the actress Silvia created many of the leading female
roles.

In 1733 L'HEUREUX STRATAGÈME (SUCCESSFUL
STRATEGIES) appeared for the Italians and in 1737 the same
company presented LA FAUSSE CONFIDENCE (FALSE
ADMISSIONS). THE DISPUTE was performed unsuccessfully by
the *Comédie-Française* in 1744, two years after Marivaux had been a
member of the Académie française. He died on February 12th, 1763.

NED CHAILLET

FALSE ADMISSIONS

FALSE ADMISSIONS received its British première in this translation at the Lyric Theatre, Hammersmith in 1983. The cast was as follows:

ARLEQUIN	Nick Dunning
DORANTE	John Price
DUBOIS	Sam Dale
MONSIEUR REMY	Philip Voss
MARTON	Maggie Wells
ARAMINTE	Holly Wilson
MADAME ARGANTE	Sandra Voe
LE COMTE	James Smith
DIRECTOR	Mike Alfreds
SET, COSTUME AND LIGHTING	Paul Dart

CHARACTERS

ARLEQUIN

DORANTE

DUBOIS

MONSIEUR REMY

MARTON

ARAMINTE

MADAME ARGANTE

LE COMTE

ACT ONE

SCENE ONE

ARLEQUIN: *(Bringing in Dorante.)* Please be so kind as to sit here for a moment. Mademoiselle Marton is with my mistress and will come down presently.

DORANTE: Thank you.

ARLEQUIN: If you wish, I'll keep you company to prevent you from feeling bored. We can talk away the time while you wait.

DORANTE: Thank you, but that's not necessary. Don't put yourself to any trouble.

ARLEQUIN: You needn't feel uneasy about that. My mistress has ordered us to behave with the utmost courtesy and you may observe that I do so.

DORANTE: I'd quite like to be alone.

ARLEQUIN: Oh, very well, suit yourself.

SCENE TWO

Dorante; Dubois comes in with an air of mystery.

DORANTE: Ah, there you are.

DUBOIS: Yes, I've been watching for you.

DORANTE: I thought I'd never be rid of the servant. Hasn't Monsieur Remy arrived yet?

DUBOIS: No, but he said he'd be here about this time. *(He looks around.)* Can anyone see us? It's imperative the servants don't find out we know each other.

DORANTE: I don't see anyone.

DUBOIS: You haven't told your uncle, Monsieur Remy, anything about our plan?

DORANTE: Not a word. It's in all innocence that he's agreed to

introduce me as a steward here. He believes I went to
him only because he is this lady's solicitor – he has no
idea it was you who told me to approach him. He
talked to her about me yesterday and told me to come
and meet her this morning. If he wasn't here, I was to
ask for a Mademoiselle Marton. That's all. And I don't
want to entrust our plan to him or to anyone else. I've
consented to take part in it, Dubois, but I still think
it's preposterous. It's not that I'm ungrateful: I know
you wish me well. Ah, Dubois, I had to let you go.
You were the best servant in the world. I was never
even able to reward you properly for your diligence.
And you're still determined to see me prosper, I'll
always be in your debt.

DUBOIS: Listen: in a word, I'm satisfied with you, I always have
              been. You're a good man, I like you, and if I had any
              money, I'd put it all at your disposal.

DORANTE: Will I ever be able to thank you? I'd share any fortune
              I had with you, but this project will lead to nothing
              more than the disgrace of being thrown out of here
              tomorrow.

DUBOIS: Well, you'll go back where you came from.

DORANTE: This woman is highly placed in the world, she sees only
              the best people, she's the widow of a very wealthy
              banker, and you still think that she'll pay attention to
              me. That I'll marry her, when I am nothing, and have
              nothing.

DUBOIS: Nothing? Your looks are a gold mine. Turn around –
              let me observe you. You must be joking! Here's a
              figure worth more than any title. We won't fail, we
              can't fail. I can see you, yes, it's late at night, the house
              is quiet and you're walking from your apartments into
              hers.

DORANTE: Idle dreams.

DUBOIS: And now, you're dressed to go out, you're waiting for
              your carriage to be brought to the door.

DORANTE: She has more than fifty thousand *livres* a year, Dubois.

DUBOIS: Ah, and you have at least sixty *livres* a year.

DORANTE: You tell me she's a woman of good sense.

DUBOIS: So much the better for you, so much the worse for her.
If she comes to like you she'll feel so ashamed, she'll
fight against it so much she'll become so exhausted
she'll have to marry you to get her strength back.
You'll tell me all about it. You've seen her and you
love her?

DORANTE: I love her passionately, that's why I'm so afraid.

DUBOIS: Enough of your terrors. Have a little confidence. I'm
taking care of this, I want it, I have it here, *(He points
to his head.)* and I tell you you'll succeed. We've
decided on what to do, everything's ready: I know my
mistress, I know your merits, I know my abilities, and
I'm guiding you. And we will love you, sensible as we
are. We will marry you, proud as we are. And we will
make you rich, poor as you are. Pride, sense, wealth, all
will succumb. When love speaks, it is a master, and
love will speak. I must leave you: here's Monsieur
Remy. We've begun, let's continue. *(He takes a few
steps and comes back.)* By the way, try to make Marton
feel some inclination for you. Love and I will take care
of the rest.

SCENE THREE

Monsieur Remy, Dorante.

M. REMY: I'm pleased to see you're punctual, dear nephew.
Mademoiselle Marton has been told you're here and is
coming. Do you know her?

DORANTE: No. Why do you ask?

M. REMY: As I was on my way here, an idea came to me . . . she's
pretty.

DORANTE: Is she?

M. REMY: And she comes from a very good family. Her father
was a solicitor and I took over his practice when he
died. He was also a good friend of your father's.
Unfortunately, he was a little careless, went into debt,
and his daughter has been left unprovided for. The

lady here took her into the house as a companion, but she treats her more as a friend than as a servant. She has promised to do something for her when she gets married. There's also an old asthmatic relation who's well off and Marton stands to inherit from her. Since you'll both be living in the same house, I think you should marry her. What do you say to that?

DORANTE: *(Smiles aside.)* Eh! . . . I wasn't thinking of her.

M. REMY: Let me suggest you start and that you try to make her like you. You have nothing, nephew, nothing more than a little hope. You're my heir, but I'm healthy and I have every intention of lasting as long as I can. And then, I might marry. I don't want to, but that kind of thing can happen suddenly: a pretty face starts the process – and there are a few of them about. Once married, one has children, that's the custom, and so much for the indirect line. So nephew, take care, and make yourself independent of an inheritance I might promise today, but withdraw tomorrow.

DORANTE: You're right, I'll work on it.

M. REMY: That's my counsel. Here's Mademoiselle Marton. I'll find out what she thinks of you.

> *Dorante moves off.*

SCENE FOUR

Monsieur Remy, Marton, Dorante.

MARTON: I'm so sorry I kept you waiting, but I was delayed by my mistress.

M. REMY: There's no harm done, I've just arrived myself. Tell me, what's your opinion of that tall young man? *(Showing Dorante.)*

MARTON: And why should I tell you, Monsieur Remy?

M. REMY: Because he's my nephew.

MARTON: I think that nephew is fit to be shown. He doesn't disgrace the family.

M. REMY: Really? I'm delighted you like him. He's the steward
               I'm presenting to your mistress. He's met you several
               times before, when you came to bring me papers. Do
               you remember?

MARTON: No, I don't.

M. REMY: We don't always notice everything. Do you know what
               he said to me the first time he saw you?
               "Who's that very pretty girl?" *(Marton smiles.)* Come
               here, my dear nephew. *(To Marton.)* Your father and
               his father loved each other, why shouldn't the children
               do the same? Here's someone who asks for nothing
               better. His heart is ready for the taking.

DORANTE: *(Embarrassed)* That shouldn't be difficult to believe.

M. REMY: See how he looks at you: you could make a worse
               transaction.

MARTON: I'm convinced: you've predisposed me in his favour.
               We'll see.

M. REMY: We'll see? I won't leave until we do see.

MARTON: *(Laughing)* I wouldn't want to go too fast.

DORANTE: You're making Mademoiselle Marton uneasy, uncle.

MARTON: *(Laughing)* Surely I don't appear too reluctant.

M. REMY: Ah, I'm so pleased you're both agreed. Oh, my
               children, *(He takes their hands.)* I leave you engaged
               and look forward to an even better event soon.
               Goodbye, dear niece, I'll let you introduce your
               intended husband to your mistress.

                     Exit.

MARTON: *(Laughing)* Goodbye, uncle.

SCENE FIVE

Marton, Dorante.

MARTON: How quickly Monsieur Remy has despatched all this –
               it's like a dream. Will your love be as lasting as it is
               sudden?

DORANTE: The one as much as the other.

MARTON: He left too soon. I hear my mistress. If you go on to the
           terrace for a moment I'll warn her you've come.
           Thanks to Monsieur Remy, your interests are almost
           mine.

DORANTE: I'll go.

MARTON: (*Watching him leave.*) These sudden feelings two people
           have for each other – how wonderful they are.

SCENE SIX

Araminte, Marton.

ARAMINTE: Marton, who's that man who bowed to me so
           gracefully. Has he come to talk to you?

MARTON: No, to you.

ARAMINTE: (*Quite animated.*) Well, let him come in. Why is he
           leaving?

MARTON: He wanted me to talk to you first. He's Monsieur
           Remy's nephew, the one proposed to you as a steward.

ARAMINTE: Ah, he's the one. He has a most agreeable manner.

MARTON: I know he is generally well thought of.

ARAMINTE: Yes, I can believe that. But Marton, he is so handsome.
           I have some qualms about taking him on. Might people
           not talk?

MARTON: Talk? Who said that stewards must be ugly?

ARAMINTE: You're right, tell him to come back in. It wasn't
           necessary to prepare me: Monsieur Remy's
           recommendation is sufficient. I'll take him.

MARTON: (*About to leave.*) You couldn't make a better choice.
           (*Coming back.*) Have you agreed on the terms of his
           contract? Monsieur Remy asked me to mention it.

ARAMINTE: We won't have any disagreements. It's obvious he's a
           man of merit. Call him.

MARTON:	And we'll give him the apartments that overlook the garden?
ARAMINTE:	Yes, yes, anything he wants. Let him come.

Marton goes off.

<u>SCENE SEVEN</u>

Dorante, Araminte, Marton.

MARTON:	Monsieur Dorante, my mistress is expecting you.
ARAMINTE:	Come in. I'm very grateful to Monsieur Remy for having done me the kindness of offering his own nephew. There was another steward who was recommended to me by a friend the day before yesterday and I was expecting him today but I'll keep you.
DORANTE:	I hope my eagerness will justify such a preference and that you won't change your mind. Nothing would pain me more.
MARTON:	It's all agreed then.
ARAMINTE:	Yes, I won't look any further. You're familiar with this kind of work? You've done it before?
DORANTE:	My father was a solicitor. I could have been one myself.
ARAMINTE:	I see that you come from a very good family and that this position must be slightly beneath you.
DORANTE:	I don't feel there's anything humiliating in such a position: it's beneath no one to have the honour of serving someone like you. I envy no one else his place.
ARAMINTE:	Nothing in my behaviour will make you change those feelings. And if, later on, I can be of any help I won't fail you.
MARTON:	How like my mistress.
ARAMINTE:	Yes, I hate to see young men of worth deprived of wealth, when there are so many nonentities about who

have fortunes. I find it even more disturbing with someone of your age: you can't be more than thirty.

DORANTE: Not quite.

ARAMINTE: It must at least be a consolation for you to know that you still have time to find happiness.

DORANTE: I began to find it today.

ARAMINTE: You'll be taken to your apartments, and if they don't suit you, you can choose others. We must also find you a servant. Who shall it be, Marton?

MARTON: What about Arlequin? He's in the hall. Arlequin, come here.

SCENE EIGHT

Araminte, Dorante, Marton, Arlequin.

ARLEQUIN: Here I am.

ARAMINTE: Arlequin, as of now you're to serve Monsieur Dorante, I'm giving you to him.

ARLEQUIN: You're giving me to him? Don't I belong to myself any more?

MARTON: What an idiot.

ARAMINTE: I mean that you'll serve him instead of serving me.

ARLEQUIN: *(As if to cry.)* I don't understand why you want to dismiss me. I'm sure I don't deserve such a treatment, I always did the best I could to serve you well.

ARAMINTE: I'm not dismissing you, I'm paying you to be with Monsieur Dorante.

ARLEQUIN: I must point out that would be very wrong of you. I can't work for one side when my money's coming from another, and if you pay my wages, you should have the benefit of my services. Otherwise, I'd be cheating you most scandalously.

ARAMINTE: I can't make him understand.

MARTON: You're really stupid! Don't you obey me when I tell
            you to go somewhere or to do something?

ARLEQUIN: Always.

MARTON: Well, now it'll be Monsieur Dorante instead of me
            who'll tell you these things. It's still on behalf of your
            mistress and by her command.

ARLEQUIN: Ah, that's a different matter altogether. My mistress is
            ordering him to suffer my services and I'm lending
            these to him by her orders.

MARTON: Exactly.

ARLEQUIN: You see that it needed explaining.

ARAMINTE: I must go and look at some materials. *(To Dorante.)* I
            have something to ask you. Don't go away.

SCENE NINE

Dorante, Marton, Arlequin.

ARLEQUIN: So, now we belong to each other, but you're one ahead
            of me. I'm the valet with orders to serve you and
            you're the valet with orders to be served.

MARTON: That buffoon with his big phrases. Go away.

ARLEQUIN: Just a moment. Aren't you going to give me
            something? Are you under orders to be served for
            nothing?

            Dorante laughs.

MARTON: Leave us. Isn't it enough that your mistress will pay
            you?

ARLEQUIN: So I'm to cost you absolutely nothing? You certainly
            couldn't get anyone cheaper.

DORANTE: Arlequin is right. Here's an advance.

ARLEQUIN: This is a gesture worthy of a master. The rest can await
            your leisure.

DORANTE: Go and drink to my health.

ARLEQUIN: If your health is to depend solely on my drinking, I
              swear it'll never fail you. *(Aside)* What a charming
              companion chance has thrown my way.

SCENE TEN

Dorante, Marton, Madame Argante (who arrives a moment later.)

MARTON: My mistress seems to think very highly of you. That's
              to our advantage. You should be pleased. But here's
              her mother, Madame Argante. I think I know what
              brings her here.

MME
ARGANTE: *(A curt and vain woman.)* So, Marton, my daughter tells
              me she's taken a steward recommended to her by her
              solicitor. I disapprove. The Comte has already found a
              steward for her and Araminte hasn't taken his feelings
              into account. She should at least have waited and seen
              them both. What does she like so much about this one,
              what sort of a man is he?

MARTON: He's here.

MME
ARGANTE: Him! That's unthinkable. He's too young.

MARTON: Thirty is old enough to be a steward.

MME
ARGANTE: That depends. Have you definitely been hired?

DORANTE: I have.

MME
ARGANTE: And where were you before?

DORANTE: At home. I haven't worked for anyone yet.

MME
ARGANTE: You were at home? And you've come here to serve
              your apprenticeship?

MARTON: Not at all. Monsieur Dorante is the son of a most
              skilful father, he knows his business.

MME ARGANTE:	*(Aside to Marton.)* I don't think very much of him. A steward shouldn't look like that.
MARTON:	Looks have nothing to do with it, he's the man we need.
MME ARGANTE:	Well, as long as he fits in with our plans, I don't mind whether we use him or another.
DORANTE:	May I ask what these are?
MME ARGANTE:	Have you heard of the Comte Dorimont? It's an illustrious name. My daughter and he are in dispute over the ownership of a considerable piece of property and are about to go to law. Clearly, the best way to avoid the lawsuit is for them to marry. My daughter is the widow of a man who was highly regarded in the world and who left her a very rich woman. But as the Comtesse Dorimont, her rank would be so exalted, she would keep company with people of such distinction, that I'm most anxious for this marriage to take place. And I must admit that I'm delighted by the notion of becoming the mother of the Comtesse Dorimont, or perhaps something even better. Nothing's beyond the reach of the Comte.
DORANTE:	Have they both agreed to this marriage?
MME ARGANTE:	Not quite yet, but my daughter must come around to it. She claims that if she did have the legal right to the property the Comte would have reason to be grateful to her. And so, she wants to wait and find out how good her case is before marrying him. But sometimes I'm afraid this might be no more than an excuse. My daughter has only one fault: she lacks ambition. She doesn't understand the appeal of the name Dorimont, or of the title Comtesse. She doesn't see how unpleasant it is to remain in the middle class. That state has lulled her to sleep, in spite of her fortune.
DORANTE:	*(Gently)* A different state might not bring her greater happiness.

MME ARGANTE:	*(Curtly)* No one is interested in what you think. Keep your vulgar little opinions to yourself, and help us, if you want to be our friend.
MARTON:	Such notions need not harm our case.
MME ARGANTE:	I never found notions of humility attractive.
DORANTE:	How do you think I can help you?
MME ARGANTE:	I want you to tell my daughter her claim to the property is weak and that she'll lose the lawsuit.
DORANTE:	I'll certainly warn her if that's the case.
MME ARGANTE:	*(Aside to Marton.)* Hum! He's not very quick. *(To Dorante.)* You're to tell her that whether her claim is good or not.
DORANTE:	But that would be reprehensible.
MME ARGANTE:	Reprehensible? I'm reprehensible? Me? I'm her mother and I'm ordering you to deceive her for her own good, do you understand? Me!
DORANTE:	I would still be deceiving her.
MME ARGANTE:	*(Aside to Marton.)* He's hopeless, we'll have to get rid of him. *(Aloud)* Goodbye, dear accountant, who doesn't know how to take anyone else into account.

She leaves.

SCENE ELEVEN

Dorante, Marton.

DORANTE:	There's a mother who's not at all like her daughter.
MARTON:	No, there's some difference between them. I'm sorry I

didn't have time to warn you about her bluntness. As you can see, she's set on this marriage. Does it matter what you say to the daughter as long as the mother backs you? It's not necessarily dishonest. No one would blame you.

DORANTE: It's still pushing her towards a decision she might otherwise not take. If I'm needed to help her to this marriage, she must be resisting it?

MARTON: It's merely idleness.

DORANTE: Please tell me the truth.

MARTON: I have good reasons for promoting this marriage, and I'm sure you'll agree with them. The Comte has promised to give me three thousand *livres* on the day the marriage contract is signed. And according to Monsieur Remy's plans this sum concerns you as well as me.

DORANTE: Listen, you're a sweet girl, but you can't possibly contemplate accepting that money.

MARTON: On the contrary, the more I contemplate it, the more I like it.

DORANTE: But you also like your mistress. If this man were to bring her unhappiness, surely you'd regret your part in it? And for such a paltry sum!

MARTON: Say what you like, I can't agree with you. What's more, the Comte is a gentleman and to worry about anything else requires a nicety I don't possess. Here's my mistress. Ponder that sum, you might develop as much of a taste for it as I have.

　　　She leaves.

DORANTE: I don't feel so bad about deceiving her now.

SCENE TWELVE

Araminte, Dorante.

ARAMINTE: You've seen my mother?

DORANTE: Yes, just a moment ago.

ARAMINTE: She told me she'd prefer to see someone else in your place.

DORANTE: So it seemed.

ARAMINTE: Yes, but you mustn't let that worry you: you suit me.

DORANTE: I have no other ambition.

ARAMINTE: I have something to ask you, but please, this must remain between ourselves.

DORANTE: I'd sooner betray myself.

ARAMINTE: Yes, I feel I can trust you. It's this: they want me to marry the Comte Dorimont in order to avoid a court case over some property I own.

DORANTE: I know. I had the misfortune to displease Madame Argante on that very subject.

ARAMINTE: How?

DORANTE: They want me to convince you that your claim is weak, whether it is or not so that you'll agree to this marriage as soon as possible. I said I couldn't do such a thing.

ARAMINTE: My mother is so frivolous. I was depending on your loyalty. Please stay that way and don't be upset by anything my mother said. I don't approve of her behaviour: was she unpleasant?

DORANTE: It doesn't matter: it's only made me that much more attached to your interests, and eager to be of service.

ARAMINTE: And that's why I don't want anyone to cause you any more distress. What's this about? I'll get angry if it goes on. They want to behave badly towards you because you've behaved so well? How dare they!

DORANTE: Please don't pay any more attention to it. You've shown me such kindness. I'm only too happy to have borne their insults.

ARAMINTE: I find your feelings admirable. Coming back to this lawsuit, if I don't marry the Comte. . . .

SCENE THIRTEEN

Dorante, Araminte, Dubois.

DUBOIS: The Marquise is feeling better *(Pretends to see Dorante with surprise.)* and thanks you . . . thanks you . . . for your concern.

              Dorante pretends to turn his head to avoid Dubois' gaze.

ARAMINTE: Good.

DUBOIS: *(Still staring at Dorante.)* I must have a word with you. It's urgent.

ARAMINTE: What is it?

DUBOIS: I can only speak to you in private.

ARAMINTE: *(To Dorante.)* I haven't finished what I had to say. Please leave us for a moment.

SCENE FOURTEEN

Araminte, Dubois.

ARAMINTE: Why did you look so surprised when you saw Dorante?

DUBOIS: It's nothing, but I can't work for you any more. I must resign my place here.

ARAMINTE: *(Surprised)* What? Just because you've seen Dorante here?

DUBOIS: Do you have any idea who it is you're dealing with?

ARAMINTE: With Monsieur Remy's nephew, my solicitor's nephew.

DUBOIS: How did he ever manage to introduce himself here?

ARAMINTE: Monsieur Remy sent him to me, to be my steward.

DUBOIS: Your steward, him! And Monsieur Remy sent him to you? Poor man, he doesn't know what he's done. That boy is a demon.

ARAMINTE: What do you mean? Do you know him?

DUBOIS: Do I know him, do I know him? I do indeed and he
           knows me as well. Didn't you notice how quickly he
           turned his head away when I came into the room?

ARAMINTE: Yes, and now it's my turn to feel surprise. Is he
           capable of doing any harm that you know of? Is he
           bad, or dishonest?

DUBOIS: He's the best man in the world and has more decency
           in him then fifty good men put together. He is integrity
           personified, and you may not find his equal anywhere.

ARAMINTE: What's the difficulty then? Why did you frighten me
           so?

DUBOIS: His only fault lies here. *(He touches his forehead.)* The
           head's no good.

ARAMINTE: His head?

DUBOIS: Yes, the head's cracked, completely cracked.

ARAMINTE: Dorante? He seemed perfectly sane to me. What proof
           do you have of his madness?

DUBOIS: What proof? I watched it seize him six months ago.
           Yes, it's six months now that he's been raving of love,
           and drifting about, quite lost, his brain consumed by
           this fever. I have good reason to know all this, I used
           to work for him. His condition, however, became so
           severe I couldn't stay with him any longer. And now
           I'll have to go away again. Aside from that he's a
           paragon.

ARAMINTE: *(Sulking a little.)* Oh, well, I won't keep him. I don't
           want someone here who's unstable. And it's probably
           for someone who isn't even worth it. Men have such
           strange fancies.

DUBOIS: I have to stop you there. No one could find fault with
           his choice. There's discernment in his madness.

ARAMINTE: It doesn't matter. I want to send him away. Do you
           by any chance know who this person is?

DUBOIS: I have the honour of seeing her every day. This person
           is you.

ARAMINTE: Me?

DUBOIS: Yes, it's you. He's done nothing but adore you for the
               past six months, and he'd gladly relinquish his life for a
               moment's contemplation of your person. Surely you've
               noticed how enthralled he looks when he speaks to you.

ARAMINTE: Yes, there did seem to be something a little out of the
               ordinary. Heavens, the poor boy.

DUBOIS: You'll never believe the extent of his madness: it's
               destroying him. He's of good family, with a pleasing
               figure, fine features, excellent manners, but he's not
               rich. And yet, there are countless women he could have
               married, who were rich and lovely. They wanted
               nothing more than to offer him their fortune, when
               they themselves deserved to have fortunes laid at their
               feet. There's one in particular who can't forget him and
               still pursues him.

ARAMINTE: *(Negligently)* Still?

DUBOIS: Yes, still! She's a very vivacious brunette but he avoids
               her. It's useless, he turns everything down. "I'd be
               deceiving them," he told me, "I can't love any of them.
               My heart is elsewhere." And sometimes there'd be a
               tear in his eye when he said this, because he knows he's
               at fault.

ARAMINTE: How unfortunate – but where has he seen me?

DUBOIS: Alas, he lost his mind one day as you were coming out
               of the Opera. It was a Friday, yes a Friday. He told
               me he saw you walking down the stairs – he followed
               you to your carriage, and discovered your name. And
               when I found him, he was still rooted to the spot,
               spellbound, in ecstasy.

ARAMINTE: This is extraordinary.

DUBOIS: I shouted at him. No answer. No one up here. Finally,
               he came to, but he was still distracted. I threw him into
               a coach and took him home. I hoped his folly would
               pass, because I was very fond of him. He was an
               excellent master. But no, his case was desperate. That
               exquisite intelligence, that cheerful disposition, that
               sweetness of temper, you'd driven them all away. And
               from then on, he spent all day long dreaming of you
               and I spent all day long spying on you.

ARAMINTE: You astound me.

DUBOIS: I even befriended one of your servants. He was a most
precise boy and could tell me everything for a bottle of
wine. "We're going to the Comédie Française", he'd
say. And I'd run home and make my report so we
could arrive there an hour early. Or: "She's visiting this
house, that house." And on that information, we'd
station a carriage in the street for the evening so that he
could watch you go in, and come out. He was inside
the coach and I was at the back, but we were both
shivering with cold because it was winter. He didn't
even notice. I had to sustain my strength by letting out
the odd oath.

ARAMINTE: Is this possible?

DUBOIS: It is indeed. In the end, I'd had enough. My health
began to fail, as did his, so I told him you had gone into
the country. He believed me and I had a little rest. But
two days later, as he was walking in the Tuileries,
mourning your departure, he saw you. When he came
back he was so angry that – gentle as he is – he wanted
to beat me. But as I didn't want him to, I had to leave
him. I then had the good fortune to find a place here,
but now he's found his way to this house, as your
steward no less. Which, I daresay, he prefers to being
Emperor.

ARAMINTE: This is all so strange. Ah, and I was so pleased to have
him, because he's honest. I'm tired of being deceived
by people. It's not that I'm angry, I'm beyond all that.

DUBOIS: You'd do him a kindness to send him away. The more
he sees you, the more he'll deteriorate.

ARAMINTE: I would send him away, but I'm not certain that would
cure him. And I don't know what to say to Monsieur
Remy. This is awkward – I don't quite see how to rid
myself of him without being rude.

DUBOIS: Yes, but you'll make his condition incurable.

ARAMINTE: (*Abruptly*) Oh, too bad, I can't manage without a
steward at the moment. I don't believe it's as
dangerous as you think. Actually, if there's one thing
that can bring him back to his senses, it is the habit of

seeing me more often. It would even be doing him
a service.

DUBOIS: I suppose it's a harmless enough remedy. At least, he'll
never whisper a word of his love.

ARAMINTE: Are you quite sure?

DUBOIS: He'd sooner die. You've made him feel such respect,
adoration, humility, it's almost inconceivable. Do you
think he dreams of being loved in return? Never.
According to him, there's no one in this world worthy
of your love. He asks for nothing more than to see you,
occasionally, and admire your eyes, your features, the
gracefulness of your figure. That's all. He told me so a
thousand times.

ARAMINTE: *(Shrugging her shoulders.)* He deserves compassion. I
should at least wait a few days until I can find another
steward. And listen, Dubois, you mustn't be uneasy,
I'm pleased with you and I'll reward you for your
diligence. You mustn't leave me, do you understand?

DUBOIS: I'm yours for life.

ARAMINTE: I'll take good care of you. Now whatever you do, don't
tell him I know his secret. Don't tell anyone, not even
Marton. This requires absolute discretion.

DUBOIS: You're the only one I've spoken to.

ARAMINTE: He's coming back, go.

SCENE FIFTEEN

Dorante, Araminte.

ARAMINTE: To tell the truth, that's an admission I could have done
without.

DORANTE: What is it you wish me to do?

ARAMINTE: Yes, what were we talking about? I've forgotten.

DORANTE: It concerned your lawsuit with the Comte.

ARAMINTE: I remember now, I was saying they want us to marry.

DORANTE: Yes, and I believe you were about to say you didn't feel inclined towards it.

ARAMINTE: That's right. I wanted you to look into the case and tell me if it was safe to take it to court. There's no need to do that now. I may not be able to keep you.

DORANTE: Ah, but you were kind enough to assure me that you would.

ARAMINTE: I'd forgotten I'd promised the Comte to take a steward he found for me. It would be uncivil to break such a promise and I must at least grant him an interview.

DORANTE: I'm unfortunate. Nothing I do seems to succeed, and now I'm even to be dismissed.

ARAMINTE: *(Weakly)* I didn't say that, nothing's been decided yet.

DORANTE: Don't leave me in such uncertainty.

ARAMINTE: I'll try to let you stay, I'll try.

DORANTE: Then you're asking me to look into this case?

ARAMINTE: Let's wait: it would be a waste of effort if I were to marry the Comte anyway.

DORANTE: I thought I heard you say you felt no inclination for him.

ARAMINTE: Not yet.

DORANTE: You have a life of such ease and tranquility.

ARAMINTE: *(Aside)* I don't have the strength to make him suffer. *(Aloud)* Well then, yes, do look into it. I have the papers in my closet. *(Leaving)* I hardly dare look at him.

SCENE SIXTEEN

Dorante, Dubois (coming in with an air of mystery, as if just passing through.)

DUBOIS: Marton is looking for you to show you your apartments, Arlequin is drinking, how are you faring?

DORANTE: How lovely she is: How did she take what you told
             her?

DUBOIS: (*As if running off.*) She's coming, little by little, to the
             conclusion that she ought to keep you out of pity. She
             believes she can effect a cure by letting you see her as
             often as you wish.

DORANTE: (*Delighted*) Does she?

DUBOIS: She won't escape now. I'm going.

DORANTE: No, stay, I see Marton. Tell her I've gone to get some
             papers.

DUBOIS: Go, I have a little something to say to Marton: it's time
             to raise doubts in everyone's mind.

SCENE SEVENTEEN

Dubois, Marton.

MARTON: Where's Dorante? Wasn't he just with you?

DUBOIS: (*Sharply*) He said he was going to get some papers.
             Why does he have to look over these apartments? If he
             didn't like them he'd be difficult to please and I'd tell
             him straight away to . . .

MARTON: It's none of your business. I'm following the
             instructions of my mistress.

DUBOIS: She's a kind and prudent woman but there's something
             about the way that steward looks at her which puts me
             in mind of a suitor.

MARTON: He looks like what he is.

DUBOIS: I'm sure I've seen the face of that little gentleman
             somewhere and it was turned towards our mistress.

MARTON: Are you always unhappy when someone finds her
             beautiful?

DUBOIS: No, but I'm beginning to wonder if he hasn't come
             here to get a closer look at her.

MARTON: *(Laughing)* Ah! Ah! What an idea. You don't
           understand a thing, you're way off the mark.

DUBOIS: *(Laughing)* Ah! Ah! I must be stupid.

MARTON: *(Laughing as she leaves.)* Ah! Ah! What a strange way of
           interpreting things.

DUBOIS: *(Alone)* You won't think it strange for long, I'll make
           sure of that. And now, let us launch the full offensive.

END OF ACT ONE

ACT TWO

SCENE ONE

Araminte, Dorante.

DORANTE: No, you won't risk anything by taking this case to court. I've consulted several people and I'm convinced you'll win. If that's your only reason for marrying the Comte, there's nothing here to force you.

ARAMINTE: He'd feel so hurt if I didn't.

DORANTE: It wouldn't be right to sacrifice yourself out of fear of hurting him.

ARAMINTE: Are you sure you've looked carefully into the case? You said to me before that my life was one of ease and tranquility. Wouldn't you prefer me to stay that way? Aren't you perhaps a little prejudiced against this marriage, and therefore against the Comte?

DORANTE: I'm not interested in him or anyone else, I care only about your well-being.

ARAMINTE: Yes, I can't criticise you for that. If I do marry the Comte and he insists on replacing you, I promise I'll find you an even better position.

DORANTE: *(Sadly)* I won't go to anyone else if I lose my place here. And I fear I will lose it.

ARAMINTE: I think I'll take this case to court after all, we'll see.

DORANTE: There's one more thing: the caretaker of one of your estates has just died. You'll probably want him replaced by someone from here. What about sending Dubois? I can easily find you another servant.

ARAMINTE: No, send your man to the Château and leave Dubois with me. He's a trustworthy lad. By the way, he told me he worked for you at one time.

DORANTE: *(Feigning unease.)* Yes, he's faithful, but not always truthful. These people rarely give a good account of

those they've served: I hope he's not prejudicing you
against me.

ARAMINTE: *(Casually)* He speaks very well of you. What does
Monsieur Remy want?

SCENE TWO

Araminte, Dorante, Monsieur Remy.

M. REMY: I've come to thank you for your kindness in accepting
my nephew.

ARAMINTE: I had no doubts, as you see.

M. REMY: I couldn't be more grateful, but didn't you say you've
been offered someone else?

ARAMINTE: I was.

M. REMY: Excellent. I need this one for something else.

DORANTE: *(With an expression of refusal.)* What's this?

M. REMY: Wait.

ARAMINTE: This is rather sudden, Monsieur Remy, and badly
timed. I've already sent the other steward away.

DORANTE: I won't leave unless I'm dismissed.

M. REMY: *(Sharply)* You don't know what you're saying. You
must leave. You'll see. *(To Araminte.)* Judge for
yourself: There's a woman of about thirty-five, who's
said to be quite pretty, from a good family, and
generally commendable. She won't give her name, but
says I've acted as her solicitor. She has fifteen thousand
a year, she can prove this. She saw Dorante at my
house, she spoke with him, she knows he's poor, and she
wants to marry him without delay. *(To Dorante.)* The
servant who brought me this message will come back for
your answer and take you directly to her house. Is that
clear? I don't see that there's anything to discuss. You
must be ready in two hours. *(To Araminte.)* Can you
find fault with anything I've said?

ARAMINTE: *(Coldly)* He must answer for himself.

M. REMY: Well, what are you waiting for? Are you coming?

DORANTE: No, Uncle, I don't wish to.

M. REMY: Hum! You haven't heard what I've just said: she has
              fifteen thousand a year, do you understand?

DORANTE: If she had twenty times that amount, I couldn't marry
              her. We wouldn't be happy, my heart is engaged
              elsewhere.

M. REMY: *(Sarcastically, in a sing-song.)* "My heart is engaged
              elsewhere." How unfortunate. Ah, ah, the heart is
              indeed an admirable instrument. Who could have
              guessed the exquisite qualms of a heart that wants you
              to remain the steward of someone else's house, when
              you could be the overseer of your own? Are those your
              final words, oh faithful shepherd?

DORANTE: I can't change my feelings.

M. REMY: What a stupid heart, nephew. You're a half-wit, a
              madman. And I believe this woman you love was
              conceived by an ape if she doesn't think the same. *(To
              Araminte.)* Don't you agree with me? Isn't his
              behaviour extraordinary?

ARAMINTE: *(Gently)* Don't quarrel with him. He could be wrong, I
              agree.

M. REMY: What? But he could be –

ARAMINTE: Yes, but from his point of view, it's understandable.
              And yet, Dorante, you must try to overcome your
              feelings. It's not easy, I know.

DORANTE: I can't: my love is dearer to me than my life.

M. REMY: *(With an astonished air.)* What satisfaction this must
              give to all those who love fine feelings. This is the
              strangest case I've ever come across. *(To Araminte.)* Is
              this a sensible way to act?

ARAMINTE: I'll let you talk to him. *(Aside)* I feel so sorry for him.

              She leaves.

DORANTE: *(Aside)* If only he knew how useful he's been.

SCENE THREE

Dorante, Monsieur Remy, Marton.

M. REMY: Do you know, Dorante, I believe you'd feel more at home in a madman's cell. *(Marton comes in.)* Come here, Mademoiselle Marton.

MARTON: I just heard you were here.

M. REMY: Come and give us your opinion: what do you make of a man who has nothing of his own and still finds it in himself to turn down a pretty, respectable woman, with a good fifteen thousand a year?

MARTON: That's not difficult: he's a fool.

M. REMY: Here's that fool. And what's his excuse? His heart! It seems you've taken possession of it, but you strike me as still being in your senses, you haven't known him for very long and I assume he hasn't yet taken yours; so you must help me lead him back to reason. You're a very pretty woman, but I'm certain you wouldn't want to prevent such an advantageous marriage. No eyes, however beautiful, deserve such a sacrifice.

MARTON: What's this? Dorante is turning down a fortune for my sake?

M. REMY: Just so. And your generosity will not allow this to happen.

MARTON: *(Passionate)* You're mistaken, Monsieur Remy. I can't prevent it when I love him so much myself. No, I'm delighted. Ah! Dorante, you're admirable. I never suspected you loved me that much!

M. REMY: Wait. I've barely shown him to you and you're already seized with passion. By God, the heart of a woman ignites quickly.

MARTON: *(As if hurt.)* Are riches that necessary to happiness? My mistress is so kind to me, she'll make up for at least part of what Dorante is sacrificing. And I, Dorante, will always feel such gratitude.

DORANTE: No, no, you mustn't. I'm the only one concerned in

this. I've only consulted my feelings, and you have
nothing to thank me for. I don't deserve your gratitude.

MARTON: Oh, Dorante, no one has ever expressed themselves
                with more delicacy and tenderness. You've captivated
                my heart.

M. REMY: I must understand nothing about these matters,
                because I find him totally insipid. *(To Marton.)*
                Goodbye, sweet child. Frankly, I wouldn't have prized
                you so highly. *(To Dorante.)* Well, fool, hold on to your
                tenderness, you've just lost your inheritance.

                He leaves.

MARTON: He's angry now, but we'll conciliate him.

DORANTE: I hope so. Someone's coming.

MARTON: It's the Comte, the one who's to marry my mistress.

DORANTE: I don't want to see him – he might try to discuss the
                lawsuit with me. You already know my thoughts on
                that subject.

SCENE FOUR

Comte, Marton.

COMTE: Ah, Marton.

MARTON: You're back.

COMTE: Yes. I heard Araminte was in the garden. Her mother
                has just told me something that distresses me. Even
                though I had found a steward for Araminte, and had
                promised to bring him here today, she's already taken
                on someone else. Her mother doesn't like this man; she
                fears he won't help us.

MARTON: He won't harm us either. Don't worry, he's a
                gentleman and Madame Argante has only herself to
                blame for not liking him. She was so rude to him, it's
                hardly surprising she didn't win him over. Just
                imagine, she quarrelled with him for being too
                handsome.

COMTE:	Did he just go out?
MARTON:	Yes.
COMTE:	His appearance is indeed very pleasing. He doesn't much look the steward.
MARTON:	He's an excellent man, I assure you.
COMTE:	Can't we make our peace with him and come to an arrangement? I know Araminte doesn't dislike me, but she's slow to decide. If she were to hear that the outcome of our dispute was doubtful, she wouldn't want the troubles of a lawsuit. I'm certain that's all she needs to make her agree to our marriage. Let's talk to this man, and if it needs only money to win him over, he can rely on me.
MARTON:	That won't work, there's not a man in the whole of France who's less interested in money.
COMTE:	Pity, such people are useless.
MARTON:	Let me take care of this.

SCENE FIVE

Comte, Arlequin, Marton.

ARLEQUIN:	I've just been with a man who was looking for another man.
MARTON:	What man? Which man did he want?
ARLEQUIN:	Ah, that's the difficulty. I don't know which man I must go to. I thought you might be able to come to my aid.
MARTON:	Idiot, explain yourself.
ARLEQUIN:	The man – that's the first man – brought a box, which had a miniature inside. He said the box had been ordered from his shop and he was to deliver it here, but he had strict instructions to give it to no one but the right man – that's the second man – that is, the man who ordered it. I told him there was absolutely no

difficulty in this, I'd find the man and deliver it safely. But he forgot to tell me who that man was.

MARTON: Is that man you?

COMTE: No, assuredly not.

ARLEQUIN: Come to think of it, he did mention a name. Yes, he said I could find him through Monsieur Remy. But he didn't say to deliver it to Monsieur Remy. So Monsieur Remy cannot be the man.

COMTE: Show us the box.

ARLEQUIN: No, I said I'd deliver it safely into the hands of the man who ordered it. There's the portrait of a lady inside.

COMTE: The portrait of a lady. Could it be of Araminte? I need only ask her, yes, I'll ask her directly.

      He leaves.

SCENE SIX

Arlequin, Marton.

MARTON: You were a fool to mention the portrait in front of him. It can only have been meant for Monsieur Dorante.

ARLEQUIN: Oh, my master's the man. Why didn't I think of that?

MARTON: Did you look at the portrait?

ARLEQUIN: No, why should I? That wouldn't have told me who it was for.

MARTON: Give it to me: I know all about it and your master won't mind if I see it. Don't you understand? The portrait is of me.

ARLEQUIN: Oh, you can have it then. And when you see my master, remind him of all the trouble I've taken to see it safely delivered.

MARTON: Yes, yes, go now.

SCENE SEVEN

Marton, Dorante.

MARTON: *(Alone for a moment.)* It can only be my portrait. What a delightful man! Monsieur Remy was right. Dorante has known me for some time.

DORANTE: Didn't I just see Arlequin? I understand someone came looking for me.

MARTON: *(Looking at him with tenderness.)* You deserve to be loved, Dorante, I would do you an injustice if I didn't. Yes, someone did come and I have the box. It's in my hands.

DORANTE: I don't understand. . .

MARTON: Why make a mystery of it? I tell you I have the box and you see that I'm not angry, I'll give it back to you when I've looked at it. Go now, I see my mistress with her mother and the Comte and they might be talking about this matter now. Leave me to reassure them.

DORANTE: *(Laughing as he leaves.)* It's working. She fell into it admirably.

SCENE EIGHT

Araminte, Comte, Madame Argante, Marton.

ARAMINTE: Marton, what's all this about a portrait which is supposed to be of me, and must only be delivered into the hands of a man who cannot be named?

MARTONA: *(With an absent air.)* It's nothing. I found out about it after the Comte left. It doesn't involve you. There's nothing here to interest you.

COMTE: How do you know? You haven't seen the portrait.

MARTON: It's just as if I had. I know the person it concerns. You need not feel alarmed.

COMTE: This much is clear: it's the portrait of a lady, the man who owns the portrait is being sought here, and I am not that man.

MARTON: Yes, but I've already told you, it doesn't involve my mistress or you.

ARAMINTE: Since you're so well informed, I should like you to tell me everything you know. I'm not happy with the suspicions that have been floating about.

MME
ARGANTE: Yes, there's a mystery here which is most disagreeable, but you mustn't get angry with the Comte, daughter. A little jealousy, even misplaced, is not unattractive in a lover.

COMTE: It is only that I envy this unknown man who has dared to give himself the pleasure of possessing your portrait.

ARAMINTE: *(With spirit.)* Perhaps, but you seemed to mean somethin quite different, and a disposition of that kind makes me fearful. Well, Marton?

MARTON: Why make such a fuss? It's a portrait of me.

COMTE: Of you?

MARTON: Yes, of me. Why shouldn't it be? Why do you look so surprised?

MME
ARGANTE: *(To the Comte.)* I find this as astounding as you do.

MARTON: I don't wish to sound vain, but there are portraits painted every day, and these women, for all their finery, are not my equal.

ARAMINTE: Who could possibly have undertaken such an expense for your sake?

MARTON: A most delightful man, who's considerate, sensitive, who loves me, and wants to marry me. Since you must know, it's Dorante.

ARAMINTE: My steward?

MARTON: Your steward.

MME
ARGANTE: Sensitive indeed.

ARAMINTE:	*(Sharply)* You're mistaken. He hasn't had the time since he's been here to have you painted.
MARTON:	He's seen me before.
ARAMINTE:	*(Abruptly)* Give me the box.
MARTON:	I haven't opened it yet, but you'll find me there.

Araminte opens it, all look.

COMTE:	I suspected as much: it's you.
MARTON:	You – it is. And I've been sadly mistaken. *(Aside)* Dubois was right after all.
ARAMINTE:	*(Aside)* And now I understand everything. *(To Marton.)* What made you believe it was your portrait?
MARTON:	Anyone else would have made the same mistake. There's Monsieur Remy, who tells me his nephew loves me and that it's his fervent wish to see us married soon. There's Dorante, who listens to this and denies nothing. Dorante then turns down a wealthy marriage in front of me and his uncle blames me for his decision. Then Arlequin brings a portrait and says it's for someone in this house. It's the miniature of a lady, and since Dorante has just rejected a fortune for my sake, I naturally conclude he's also had my portrait painted. Was I wrong? It seems I was. I shouldn't have expected such an honour, it was never meant for me. And now I realise how far I've been mislead, I'll keep quiet.
ARAMINTE:	I see through everything now. You're pretending to feel surprised and angry, Comte, and some of your plans have gone a little awry, but you don't deceive me. The portrait was meant for you and the man they were looking for is none other than you.
MARTON:	*(Looking serious.)* I don't think so.
MME AARGANTE:	Yes, yes, of course, it's you. Why do you wish to deny it? Given the terms you're on with my daughter, it's not a crime.
COMTE:	*(Coldly)* I assure you, on my honour, it had nothing to

do with me. Why should anyone think to find me
through Monsieur Remy? I don't even know him.

MME
ARGANTE: That's a circumstance I'd overlooked.

ARAMINTE: What's a mere circumstance? I'm still convinced. In
              any case, this portrait will go to no one, because I'm
              keeping it. What's that noise? Go and see, Marton.

SCENE NINE

Araminte, Comte, Madame Argante, Marton, Dubois, Arlequin.

ARLEQUIN: *(Coming in.)* You're vile and a lout.

MARTON: What's the matter, you two?

DUBOIS: One word from me and you'll see your master thrown
              out of here in an instant.

ARLEQUIN: Go back and live with your own kind of rabble.

DUBOIS: If it weren't for the respect I have for my mistress, I'd
              give you a good beating.

ARLEQUIN: Try it, go on, try it, she's here.

ARAMINTE: What are you quarrelling about?

MME
ARGANTE: Come here, Dubois. What's this one word you can say
              against Dorante?

ARLEQUIN: Just you dare say one word.

ARAMINTE: Quiet, let him speak.

DUBOIS: He's been abusing me like this for an hour.

ARLEQUIN: I'm paid to look after the interests of my master, and I
              can't allow this Ostrogoth to threaten him with a word.
              (To Araminte.) Am I not right to behave this way?

MME
ARGANTE: We really should hear what Dubois means by that one
              word.

ARLEQUIN: I dare you to bring out the first syllable.

DUBOIS: That was just a threat I made in a moment of anger, but I can tell you what we were quarrelling about. As I was arranging the apartments of Monsieur Dorante, I came across a painting of you. *(To Araminte.)* It didn't seem a proper place for it to hang and I decided to remove it. I was taking it down when this worm tried to stop me and we almost came to blows.

ARLEQUIN: How can you think of taking away a lovely painting which gives my master such joy. If only you'd seen with what rapture he was contemplating it before you came in. How can you be such a brute as to want to deprive my good master of what gives him so much pleasure? What spite! Take away any other object, but leave the painting, Barbarian!

DUBOIS: It will not be left there. I'll take it down myself and all your efforts will have been wasted because my mistress will agree with me.

ARAMINTE: I don't care one way or the other. What a fuss over an old canvas that's been forgotten there. It's not worth talking about.

MME
ARGANTE: *(In a sour tone.)* I'm sorry, but that is not the right place for it and it must be removed. Your steward will survive without his contemplations.

ARAMINTE: *(Sarcastically, smiling.)* I daresay he won't miss them. *(To Arlequin.)* Go away, both of you.

SCENE TEN

Araminte, Comte, Madame Argante, Marton.

COMTE: *(Sarcastically)* This much is clear: your business man is revealing himself to be a man of taste.

ARAMINTE: *(Ironically)* You're right: To have looked at a painting does indeed manifest the most extraordinary behaviour.

MME
ARGANTE: I never liked that man, daughter, and you know how perceptive I am. And now there's Dubois' threat. We

must get to the bottom of this. Let's question him.
This fine little gentleman isn't in the least suitable for
you, we all see that. Only you remain deceived.

MARTON: I'm not satisfied with him myself.

ARAMINTE: What is it that you all see and I don't? I'm totally
confused. I can't understand why I should get rid of a
man who came well recommended, well connected, and
who serves me well, perhaps only too well. That at least
doesn't confuse me.

MME
ARGANTE: You're blind.

ARAMINTE: *(Smiling)* Am I? Each goes by his own lights. I agree to
listen to Dubois. You can go and tell him I want to see
him, Marton. *(Marton leaves.)* If he can give me good
reasons to dismiss a steward who had the boldness to
look at a painting, he won't stay long. If not, I'll keep
him until I feel differently – if you please.

MME
ARGANTE: *(Crossly)* You will feel differently. I won't say any more
at present. We'll wait for better evidence.

COMTE: All I can say is that I feared he'd do me a disservice by
letting you go to court against me. And the tender
feelings I have for you made me hope that he would
dissuade you from such a course. He can do what he
likes now, I've decided that – whatever happens – I
won't let our case go to court. I'll allow you and your
business people to arbitrate: I'd rather lose everything
than quarrel with you.

MME
ARGANTE: What quarrel? Marriage will end it, and yours is
imminent.

COMTE: I won't say any more about Dorante, I'll only come
back to hear your views. If you've decided to dismiss
him, as I'm certain you will, the steward I found for
you will be at your disposal. I'll keep him a few more
days.

MME
ARGANTE: I won't say any more either, you'll accuse me of

imagining things. You'll come around to our point of
view without our help – I have faith in Dubois. We'll
leave you with him.

SCENE ELEVEN

Dubois, Araminte.

DUBOIS: Do you want to speak to me?

ARAMINTE: Come here. You're very careless, Dubois, and I
             thought so highly of you. You haven't paid any
             attention to what I said. I told you not to let anyone
             know about Dorante. You knew what absurd
             consequences it could have. So why did you quarrel
             over an old painting with an idiot who was bound to
             make an outcry, and give everyone ideas – just what I
             didn't want.

DUBOIS: I didn't know it would do any harm. I acted only out
             of respect and concern for you.

ARAMINTE: I don't need your concern, I need your silence if I'm to
             get out of this awkward situation, which is of your
             making. If it weren't for you, I wouldn't even know
             this man loves me and I wouldn't feel so involved.

DUBOIS: It was wrong of me.

ARAMINTE: Leaving aside your quarrel, how could you exclaim,
             "one word from me and my master will be thrown out."
             How could you be so clumsy?

DUBOIS: Once again, too much misplaced concern.

ARAMINTE: Well, keep quiet then, keep quiet. If only I could make
             you forget what you told me.

DUBOIS: I'm reformed.

ARAMINTE: And now, because of your blunder, I have to pretend
             to ask you about him. My mother and the Comte
             expect astonishing revelations. What shall I tell them?

DUBOIS: That's easy. Tell them I've heard that he'll be useless
             for the kind of work you require, although he's more
             than competent. Yes, ability is not what he lacks.

ARAMINTE: There's a problem with that: if he's incompetent, I'll be
            told to dismiss him and it's not the right moment for
            that. I've thought about it and I feel I must go gently
            with such an excessive passion. He might lose control
            in a moment of pain. I can't rely on a desperate man.
            I'm no longer keeping him here because I need him,
            but to protect myself. *(More softly.)* Unless Marton is
            right, in which case, I have nothing to fear. She claims
            Dorante saw her at the house of Monsieur Remy and
            has loved her for a long time. Monsieur Remy told her
            this in front of Dorante. He wants them to marry. That
            would please me.

DUBOIS: Nonsense. Dorante's never seen Marton before.
            Monsieur Remy invented that to promote their
            marriage. Dorante told me he didn't dare disabuse
            Marton. "She might," he said "become my enemy and
            turn her mistress against me. And now she's convinced
            that it's for her sake I've turned down fifteen thousand
            a year."

ARAMINTE: *(Offhand)* He said all this to you?

DUBOIS: Just now, in the garden. He wanted to throw himself at
            my feet and make me swear not to breathe a word of
            his secret passion. He begged forgiveness for his
            behaviour towards me. I told him I would keep quiet,
            but that I couldn't live in the same house with him,
            and he must leave at once. He cried, he moaned, he
            was in a very sorry state.

ARAMINTE: Ah! Don't torment him any more, you see how right I
            was to go gently with him. And I had such high hopes
            of marrying him to Marton. I thought he'd forget me
            but it seems it's not to be.

DUBOIS: A likely tale! Is there anything else?

ARAMINTE: Wait, what am I to do? If he spoke to me, I could
            complain of him. But he won't, and I know nothing
            more of his love than what you've told me, and that's
            not enough to dismiss him. Of course, if he did speak,
            it would make me angry – but that would be a good
            thing.

DUBOIS: You're right: Monsieur Dorante isn't worthy of you.

It would be a different matter if he were a rich man, because his birth is as good as any. But his only riches are his virtues and that's not sufficient.

ARAMINTE: *(In a sad tone.)* No, it isn't, that's how things are. I don't know what to do with him. I don't know. I'll see.

DUBOIS: Why don't you use the miniature as a pretext? The one Marton believed was of her.

ARAMINTE: I can't accuse him. It's the Comte who had it painted.

DUBOIS: It's not. It's Dorante. I know that because he was still working on it when I left him two months ago.

ARAMINTE: Go away, I've been talking to you too long. If anyone asks what I've found out I'll tell them what we're agreed on. Here he is, I might set him a trap.

DUBOIS: Do that: he might declare his love and then I can say to him: Out.

ARAMINTE: Leave us.

SCENE TWELVE

Dorante, Araminte, Dubois.

DUBOIS: *(As he leaves passes rapidly by Dorante.)* I can't tell him what's happened, but whether he declares himself or not, all must go well.

DORANTE: I must ask for your protection. I'm worried and unhappy: I left everything for the privilege of working for you, I can't tell you how much it means to me. No one could wish to serve you with more honesty and devotion. Despite that, I fear I may not be allowed to stay. Everyone here dislikes me, harasses me and is plotting to get rid of me. I'm dismayed and I fear you'll give into their enmity – I couldn't bear it.

ARAMINTE: *(Gently)* You mustn't feel so uneasy, you don't depend on those who dislike you. They haven't changed my opinion of you and all their little plots will come to nothing. I'm the mistress.

DORANTE: *(Looking very worried.)* I have no one but you.

ARAMINTE: And I won't fail you, but let me advise you not to look
             so apprehensive. It may make them question your
             abilities. They'll think I've kept you out of kindness.

DORANTE: They're not mistaken. No one's more aware of your
             kindness than I am.

ARAMINTE: Yes, but there's no reason for them to know about it.
             I'm grateful for your devotion, but you ought to mask
             it. That's probably what they hold against you. They
             knew you refused to deceive me over the lawsuit. Agree
             now to do what they ask and win them back that way. I
             allow you to do that and we'll let them believe you
             helped me to my decision. I've thought about it, I've
             decided to marry the Comte.

DORANTE: *(In a worried tone.)* You've decided.

ARAMINTE: Yes, I've quite made up my mind. The Comte will
             think you helped me. I'll even guarantee your place by
             telling him that. Yes, I promise you can stay. *(Aside)*
             He's changed colour.

DORANTE: What a difference that'll make for me.

ARAMINTE: *(Resolute)* No, it won't. Why should it? I'll dictate a
             letter, you'll find what you need on the table.

DORANTE: A letter. For whom?

ARAMINTE: For the Comte. He was dispirited when he left the
             house, and this note will delight him. *(Dorante remains
             distracted and does not go towards the table.)* Why don't
             you sit at the table? What are you thinking of?

DORANTE: *(Still distracted.)* Yes.

ARAMINTE: *(Aside as he sits down.)* He doesn't know what he's
             doing.

DORANTE: *(Aside, looking for paper.)* Dubois has deceived me.

ARAMINTE: *(Continuing)* Are you ready?

DORANTE: I can't find any paper.

ARAMINTE: *(Going to the table.)* You can't find any paper? It's in
             front of you.

DORANTE: So it is.

ARAMINTE: Write: "Please come soon. Your marriage is assured . . ." Have you written that?

DORANTE: Have I. . . ?

ARAMINTE: Aren't you listening? "Your marriage is assured. Madame Araminte has requested me to write you this note, but you will hear it for yourself when you come." *(Aside)* He's in pain, but he says nothing. I wonder if he will speak. "Please do not think this decision was in any way influenced by uncertainty over the outcome of the lawsuit."

DORANTE: There are no doubts, I told you you would win it.

ARAMINTE: It doesn't matter, please finish: "No, it is only the recognition of your merits that has brought this about."

DORANTE: *(Aside)* Heavens! All's lost. *(Aloud)* But you felt nothing for him.

ARAMINTE: Finish the letter, please. "It is only the recognition of your merits that has brought this about." I think your hand's shaking. What's come over you? Are you ill?

DORANTE: I don't feel very well. . . .

ARAMINTE: So suddenly, how strange. Fold the letter and address it to: The Comte Dorimont. Ask Dubois to deliver it. *(Aside)* My heart's beating. Look, this address is hardly legible. *(Aside)* And he still won't speak.

DORANTE: *(Aside)* Is she testing me? Dubois didn't warn me.

SCENE THIRTEEN

Araminte, Dorante, Marton.

MARTON: I'm glad Monsieur Dorante is here. He can confirm what I'm about to say. You've offered several times to help me when I married, but until now, I was never in a position to accept your kind offer. Today, I am wanted in marriage, and a much wealthier woman than I will ever be has just been turned down, for my sake.

At least, that's what I've been led to believe. You must make yourself clear. And as I don't want to do anything without your approval, it is from you that my hand must be obtained. *(To Dorante.)* Please speak to my mistress, if she gives you her consent, you'll have no difficulty in winning mine.

SCENE FOURTEEN

Dorante, Araminte.

ARAMINTE: *(Aside, moved.)* The fool! *(Aloud)* I'm delighted by what I've just heard. You've made a good choice: she's a lovely girl, with an excellent disposition.

DORANTE: *(With a dejected air.)* She was never in my thoughts.

ARAMINTE: Never in your thoughts but she says that you love her, that you knew her before.

DORANTE: *(Sadly)* Monsieur Remy made her believe that without consulting me. I didn't have the courage to deny it because I knew she was close to you and I was afraid of making an enemy of her. It's the same with this advantageous marriage. It wasn't I who made her believe I turned it down for her sake. I'm not in a state to give my heart to anyone, I've lost it forever, and the most glittering fortune would not tempt me.

ARAMINTE: You were wrong. You ought to have told Marton the truth.

DORANTE: She could have prevented you from seeing me. I would have thought my indifference spoke for itself.

ARAMINTE: Why, in your situation, did you feel it was so important to come into my house? Why prefer it to another?

DORANTE: I feel content here.

ARAMINTE: This is baffling. How often do you see the person you love?

DORANTE: *(Still dejected.)* Not as often as I wish. And if I saw her all the time, I would still feel it was not enough.

ARAMINTE: *(Aside)* With what tenderness he expresses himself. *(Aloud)* Is she single? Has she been married?

DORANTE: She's a widow.

ARAMINTE: Why don't you marry her? She must love you?

DORANTE: She hasn't the least suspicion that I adore her. Forgive me for speaking with such enthusiasm, I can't think of her without rapture.

ARAMINTE: I'm only asking you these questions because you've surprised me so. You say she has no idea that you love her, and yet you sacrifice a fortune for her sake. That's to be marvelled at. How can you keep such love silent? It seems to me one tries to make oneself loved in return; it's natural and forgiveable.

DORANTE: Heaven forbid I should ever conceive the smallest hope that she should love me! Me! No, no, she's too far above me, respect will keep me silent, always. At least I can look forward to dying without having had the misfortune of causing her a moment's displeasure.

ARAMINTE: I can't conceive of a woman who deserves such a passion, no, I really can't conceive of one. Is she so incomparable?

DORANTE: Don't ask me to describe her, I wouldn't know how to begin her praises. She's all that's grace and loveliness, and she can not speak to me or look at me without each time increasing my love.

ARAMINTE: *(Lowers her eyes and continues.)* But your behaviour goes against all reason. What do you expect from this love if she's never to know about it? This is strange indeed. What do you expect?

DORANTE: I ask for nothing more than to see her occasionally and to spend a little time with her.

ARAMINTE: How can you spend time with her? Have you forgotten that you're here?

DORANTE: I meant with her portrait when I can't see her.

ARAMINTE: You've had her portrait painted?

DORANTE: No, but I learnt how to paint, once, for amusement, and I made a miniature of her myself. I would have done without, rather than ask someone else to paint it.

ARAMINTE: *(Aside)* I must push him all the way. *(Aloud)* Show me this portrait.

DORANTE: Please don't ask such a thing of me. I may be without hope, but I still owe her secrecy.

ARAMINTE: I found a portrait here by chance. *(Showing the box.)* Perhaps this is it?

DORANTE: It couldn't be.

ARAMINTE: *(Opening the box.)* Yes, that would be quite extraordinary. Look carefully.

DORANTE: Please remember I would have died a thousand deaths rather than admit to you what chance has just revealed. How can I atone for . . . *(He falls to his knees.)*

ARAMINTE: I won't be angry, Dorante, I pity your distress. Please come to your senses, I forgive you.

MARTON: *(Appears and runs off.)* Ah!

> Dorante gets up quickly.

ARAMINTE: Heaven! It's Marton, she saw us.

DORANTE: *(Pretending to be disconcerted.)* No, no, she didn't come in.

ARAMINTE: I tell you she saw you. Leave me, go away, I can't bear the sight of you. Give me back my letter. *(When he's gone.)* That's what comes of keeping him.

SCENE FIFTEEN

Araminte, Dubois.

DUBOIS: Has Dorante declared himself? Can I go and talk to him?

ARAMINTE: No, he didn't say a word and there was absolutely nothing in his behaviour that even came close to anything you've described. I don't want to hear any more about it, don't meddle any further.

She leaves.

DUBOIS: We've come to the crisis.

SCENE SIXTEEN

Dubois, Dorante.

DORANTE: Ah! Dubois.

DUBOIS: Go away.

DORANTE: I don't know what to think of the conversation I've just had with her.

DUBOIS: What are you thinking of? She's not far. Do you want to ruin everything?

DORANTE: You must appease. . . .

DUBOIS: Go into the garden.

DORANTE: A doubt. . . .

DUBOIS: Into the garden, I said. I'll meet you there.

DORANTE: But. . . .

DUBOIS: I won't listen any more.

DORANTE: I'm more afraid than ever.

END OF ACT TWO

ACT THREE

SCENE ONE

Dorante, Dubois.

DUBOIS: No, let's not waste any more time. Is the letter ready?

DORANTE: I have it here, it's addressed to the rue du Figuier.

DUBOIS: And you're sure Arlequin doesn't know that area.

DORANTE: He said he didn't.

DUBOIS: You told him to ask me or Marton where it was?

DORANTE: Yes, and I'll remind him.

DUBOIS: Go and give him the letter then. I'll find Marton and take care of the rest.

DORANTE: Listen, I have some doubts. Aren't we moving too fast for Araminte? She's already in a state of such agitation, and now you want to embarrass her further by suddenly bringing everything out into the open?

DUBOIS: She must be given no quarter. She's stunned and now's the time to strike the final blow. She no longer knows what she's doing, she even lied to me by pretending you hadn't spoken of your love to her. Ha! I'll teach her to cut out my role as confidant so that she can love you in secret.

DORANTE: That last conversation was so painful. Why didn't you warn me she'd try to force me to declare myself?

DUBOIS: Do you think she wouldn't have noticed? Anyway, it made your unhappiness seem that much more real. Are you regretting the effect it had? So you felt some pain! It seems to me the event is worth a few moments of uneasiness.

DORANTE: I know what will happen: She'll suddenly decide to send me away.

DUBOIS: Let her try! No, the time when she could have acted with firmness is past. She must marry us.

DORANTE: Do be careful, her mother's wearing her down.

DUBOIS:	I wouldn't want her mother to leave her in peace.
DORANTE:	She was so ashamed when Marton found me at her feet.
DUBOIS:	Ah, really, ashamed? That's nothing, there's much more to come. I sent Marton myself when I saw where the conversation was leading.
DORANTE:	Araminte said she couldn't bear the sight of me.
DUBOIS:	She's right. How can she feel kindly towards a man she must love in spite of herself. Is that pleasant? You've taken possession of her goods, of her heart, and she's not to protest? Stop arguing, and let yourself be guided.
DORANTE:	Remember, I love her. If we fail because of this hurry, I'll be a desperate man.
DUBOIS:	I know you love her and that's why I'm not listening to you. Are you in a fit state to decide anything? This must be handled by a man with his wits about him. Ah, here's Marton, just in time. I'll keep her until you send Arlequin this way.

Dorante leaves.

SCENE TWO

Dubois, Marton.

MARTON:	*(Looking sad.)* I was looking for you.
DUBOIS:	What can I do for you?
MARTON:	Ah, Dubois, you warned me.
DUBOIS:	About what? I can't remember what I warned you about.
MARTON:	That this steward had his eyes on my mistress.
DUBOIS:	You must be talking about the expression I saw in his eyes when he looked at her. Yes, I never forgot it, that expression did not bode well.
MARTON:	We must rid ourselves of this man, Dubois.

DUBOIS: I'm doing my best. I've already told my mistress I'd heard he didn't understand much about money matters.

MARTON: But isn't there something else you know about him? I'm speaking on behalf of Madame Argante and the Comte. We think you may not have told your mistress everything or that she herself is keeping something from us. You'll have no cause to regret telling us all you know.

DUBOIS: I only know about his incompetence, and I've already told her that.

MARTON: Don't hide anything.

DUBOIS: Me! Hide something! Me! Keep a secret. I'm even less discreet than a woman. Forgive the comparison, I just wanted to set your mind at ease.

MARTON: It's obvious that he loves her.

DUBOIS: No doubt about that. I've already told her my thoughts on the subject.

MARTON: What did she say?

DUBOIS: That I was a fool. She's so partial to him.

MARTON: I wouldn't like to think how far her partially might lead her.

DUBOIS: Oh, I understand you very well.

MARTON: You seem to know more about this than I do, Dubois.

DUBOIS: I don't, I swear. But listen, Monsieur Dorante has asked Arlequin to deliver a letter for him - if we could only get hold of it, we might find out something more.

MARTON: A letter. Yes. We mustn't neglect anything. I'll go and see if Arlequin hasn't left yet.

DUBOIS: No need to go far.

SCENE THREE

Marton, Dubois, Arlequin.

ARLEQUIN: Ah, there you are, you eyesore.

DUBOIS: If I looked like you, I wouldn't laugh at others.

MARTON: What do you want, Arlequin?

ARLEQUIN: Do you by any chance know where the rue du Figuier
               is to be found?

MARTON: I do.

ARLEQUIN: It's because my dear companion, the one I have orders
               to serve, wants me to take a letter to someone who lives
               in that street, but I don't know how to find it, so he
               told me I could get that information from you. Or from
               that toad over there. But I couldn't bring myself to say
               anything to that toad that wasn't an insult. I'd rather
               see all the streets in Paris taken away by the devil than
               ask that lout how to find one of them.

DUBOIS: (Aside to Marton.) Take the letter. (Aloud) Don't tell
               him anything, let him tire himself.

ARLEQUIN: Will you be quiet!

MARTON: (Offhand) Dubois, don't interrupt. Give me the letter.
               I'm sending for something in that area and I can have
               it delivered.

ARLEQUIN: Ah! What a relief, you're a good girl.

DUBOIS: (Leaving) Yes, and thanks to your good heart, that lazy
               dog can avoid exerting himself.

ARLEQUIN: Rustic! Go and watch the painting laugh at you.

MARTON: (Alone with Arlequin.) Don't take any notice of him and
               give me the letter.

ARLEQUIN: Here. You've done me an excellent turn and if I can
               ever trot somewhere for you, don't call on anyone else.

MARTON: I'll have the letter delivered promptly.

ARLEQUIN: Yes, by all means, promptness above all. My master
               deserves promptness and every other faithful service.

MARTON: (Aside) The rascal.

ARLEQUIN: (Leaving) Don't forget I'm always at your service.

MARTON: Goodbye.

ARLEQUIN: *(Coming back.)* If you see my master, please don't tell him someone else is running in my place.

SCENE FOUR

Madame Argante, Comte, Marton.

MARTON: *(Alone for a moment.)* I won't say anything until I've seen what's in this.

MME
ARGANTE: Well, Marton, what have you learned from Dubois?

MARTON: No more than what you already know, and that's not enough.

MME
ARGANTE: Dubois is a deceitful scoundrel.

COMTE: It's clear his threat meant more than that.

MME
ARGANTE: I've sent for Monsieur Remy, and if he doesn't rid us of this steward, my daughter will have to be told he has the insolence to love her. We have the strongest indications of it and she'll have to dismiss him, if only to maintain the proprieties. I've also had the Comte's steward sent for. He's here now and I'll introduce him to her without delay.

MARTON: I don't think you'll succeed without more evidence against him. But I may have his notice in my hands at this very moment, yes, I . . . Here's Monsieur Remy, I'll go and unravel this matter.

She tries to leave.

SCENE FIVE

Monsieur Remy, Madame Argante, Comte, Marton.

M. REMY: *(To Marton as she leaves.)* Hello, dear niece, since niece you must be. Do you know why I'm wanted here?

MARTON:	*(Curtly)* Look for your niece elsewhere, Monsieur Remy, I don't like jokes in poor taste.
	She leaves.
M. REMY:	There's a discourteous young lady. *(To Madame Argante.)* I understand you sent for me. What is it about?
MME ARGANTE:	*(In a cantankerous tone.)* So, you're the solicitor.
M. REMY:	All the evidence points to that fact.
MME ARGANTE:	And what were you ever thinking of when you landed us with this steward of yours.
M. REMY:	May I ask what objections there might be to this steward.
MME ARGANTE:	Yes, we would have managed better without him.
M. REMY:	You must be quite particular not to like him.
MME ARGANTE:	He's your nephew, I hear.
M. REMY:	He is indeed.
MME ARGANTE:	Well, nephew or not, we must ask you to rid us of him.
M. REMY:	It wasn't you he was offered to.
MME ARGANTE:	No, but I don't like him, nor does the Comte, who will soon be marrying my daughter.
M. REMY:	*(Raising his voice.)* That's news. But since he's not working for you, there can be no necessity for you to like him. That detail was not part of the original agreement, and as long as Madame Araminte is satisfied with him, no one else has a right to complain. What's all this!
MME ARGANTE:	You express yourself with a certain arrogance, Monsieur Remy.

M. REMY: Your compliments have put it there, Madame Argante.

COMTE: Gently, my dear solicitor, gently. I believe you're in the wrong.

M. REMY: As you wish, my dear Comte, as you wish. But you're not concerned in any of this business. We have not been introduced and therefore can have nothing to do with each other.

COMTE: Whether we have anything to do with each other or not, Madame Argante must still approve of your nephew. She's not a stranger in this house.

M. REMY: Ah, but she's a stranger in this business, a total stranger. Dorante is completely trustworthy: as such he is known by all, as such I'll answer for him, and he is not to be spoken of in this disgraceful manner.

MME
ARGANTE: Your Dorante is insolent.

M. REMY: Nonsense. Such a word loses its meaning in your mouth.

MME
ARGANTE: In my mouth? Does this clerk know to whom he's talking? Comte, you must silence him.

M. REMY: Silence me! A solicitor! My dear lady, I've been talking for fifty years.

MME
ARGANTE: Then you've wasted fifty years of everyone's time.

SCENE SIX

Araminte, Madame Argante, Monsieur Remy, Comte.

ARAMINTE: It sounds as if you're quarrelling.

M. REMY: It would be false to say we were in harmony. You've arrived just in time. It concerns Dorante. Are you unhappy with him?

ARAMINTE: No, why should I be?

M. REMY: And have you noticed anything that might indicate he's dishonest?

ARAMINTE: I can't think of anyone more worthy of esteem.

M. REMY: According to Madame Argante, he's a scoundrel and it's my duty to free you of his presence. He's not wanted here, he's rude, he's insolent, and he's strongly disliked both by this lady here and this gentleman – who speaks with the authority of a future husband. And it seems that I only defend him because I'm senile.

ARAMINTE: (*Coldly*) I have no part in such excessive conduct, Monsieur Remy, I could never be so rude. The best I can say in Dorante's defence is that I'm keeping him. In fact I came to find out why a steward has just been brought into this house by the Comte: surely there's some mistake.

COMTE: It's true that he came here with me, but it was Madame Argante. . . .

MME ARGANTE: Yes, it was I who sent for him so that he could take the place of this other one, who will be shown the door. I know what I'm saying. I allowed your solicitor to talk, but he is embroidering.

M. REMY: Patience!

MME ARGANTE: (*Angrily*) Quiet, you've said enough. (*To Araminte.*) I didn't say his nephew was a scoundrel. Not that it's unthinkable, no, it wouldn't surprise me at all.

M. REMY: An unfortunate aside, if I may say so, betraying a strong bias and thus discrediting the evidence of the witness.

MME ARGANTE: He may be honest. At least, we don't yet have proof to the contrary, but he's still insolent, extremely insolent. I know what I'm saying, you will not keep him.

ARAMINTE: (*Cold*) He'll stay, I assure you.

MME ARGANTE:	No, he won't. You couldn't possibly keep a steward who loves you.

M. REMY:	Perhaps he ought to love you?

ARAMINTE:	Why should my steward hate me?

MME ARGANTE:	Don't equivocate. When I say he loves you, I mean that he's in love with you. He's a lover, he yearns for you, you're the secret object of his tenderness.

M. REMY:	*(Surprised)* Dorante?

ARAMINTE:	*(Laughing)* The secret object of his tenderness? Oh, yes, it's so secret as to be totally unnoticeable. I never imagined that to see me was so fraught with danger. But how is it you haven't discovered this in everyone who works here? They may all love me, who knows? Monsieur Remy, you see me often enough, don't you also love me?

M. REMY:	I must say that, were I my nephew's age, I wouldn't escape any more successfully than they say he has.

MME ARGANTE:	This is no laughing matter. We're not talking about Monsieur Remy, we can keep the poor old man out of this. Let's be serious now. All those others who work here have not had your portrait painted, they are not caught staring at a canvas of you, and they don't throw you forlorn looks.

M. REMY:	*(To Araminte.)* I let 'poor old man' pass because of you, but 'poor old man' is harsh indeed.

ARAMINTE:	Really, mother, you'd be the first to laugh at me if I took anything you've said seriously. It would be childish to dismiss Dorante because I suspect he loves me. And if no one can look at me without loving me, I suppose I'll have to get used to it. But as I've never noticed these forlorn looks I can hardly complain to Dorante about them. Furthermore, it would be eccentric to get angry with him because he has agreeable features. I'm no different from anyone else: I like handsome people.

SCENE SEVEN

Araminte, Madame Argante, Monsieur Remy, Comte, Dorante.

DORANTE: I'm sorry to interrupt you, but I have reason to believe you no longer find my services acceptable and I must ask you what is to be my fate.

MME
ARGANTE: His fate! A steward with a fate. How touching.

M. REMY: And why shouldn't he have a fate?

ARAMINTE: *(With spirit to her mother.)* Will you let me speak? *(To Dorante.)* What's made you believe you're no longer wanted here?

DORANTE: You know perfectly well: there's someone here who's come to take my place.

ARAMINTE: You're under a false impression: it wasn't I who asked him to come here.

DORANTE: Ah, I couldn't know. Mademoiselle Marton has just told me that I won't remain here an hour longer.

ARAMINTE: Marton spoke nonsense.

MME
ARGANTE: An hour longer is too long, he ought to have left an hour ago.

M. REMY: *(As if to himself.)* Let's see where all this is leading.

ARAMINTE: You mustn't feel uneasy, Dorante. I'd keep you now, even if you were the most unsuitable man in the world. I've been subjected to the most offensive proceedings. Those who brought that other man here without consulting me will be so kind as to take him away and never mention him again.

SCENE EIGHT

Araminte, Madame Argante, Monsieur Remy, Comte, Dorante, Marton.

MARTON: *(Coldly)* Don't send him away too quickly. I have a letter of recommendation for him and it was written by Monsieur Dorante himself.

ARAMINTE: What are you talking about?

MARTON: *(Giving the letter to the Comte.)* Just a moment: this deserves to be heard. As I said it was written by your steward.

COMTE: *(Reads aloud.)* "I beg you, dear friend, to be at home tomorrow morning at nine. I have so much to say to you. I believe I shall soon have to leave this house and the lady I spoke to you about. She can no longer remain ignorant of my unhappy passion, a passion which has proved incurable."

MME ARGANTE: A passion, no less! Did you hear, daughter?

COMTE: *(Reads)* "A tradesman made the unfortunate mistake of delivering a box, for the portrait I painted of her."

MME ARGANTE: We have here a character who even knows how to paint.

COMTE: *(Reads)* "I was not expecting him. He gave it to the maid."

MME ARGANTE: *(To Marton.)* A maid: that's you.

COMTE: *(Reads)* "Everyone suspects the portrait belongs to me and I fear all will be discovered. Not only must I endure the pain of being dismissed, and lose forever the pleasure of seeing every day the woman I adore . . ."

MME ARGANTE: The woman I adore! Ah! The woman I adore.

COMTE: *(Reads)* ". . . But I must also suffer her contempt."

MME ARGANTE: At least he has that right.

COMTE: *(Reads)* "This, not because of my lack of means – she would not be capable of that kind of contempt."

MME ARGANTE: Why not?

COMTE:	(*Reads*) "But because next to her, I'm worth so little, however highly others might hold me in their esteem."
MME ARGANTE:	What could possibly make them do that?
COMTE:	(*Reads*) "There is nothing left for me in Paris. And as you're about to set sail, I've decided to come with you."
MME ARGANTE:	Bon voyage.
M. REMY:	To go to sea, for this!
MME ARGANTE:	Well, daughter, what more do you need.
COMTE:	Nothing could be clearer.
ARAMINTE:	This letter isn't a forgery? You don't deny that you wrote it?
DORANTE:	I. . . .
ARAMINTE:	Leave us.

Dorante leaves.

M. REMY:	Well! So? It's a case of love. It's not the first time a beautiful face has induced it. On the other hand, he didn't feel any for those other women who would have been only too happy to return it. There's nothing wrong with this love but the fact that it's costing him fifteen thousand a year, not to mention driving him to sea. If he were a wealthy man, (*Imitating Madame Argante.*) this 'character' would be as suitable as anyone else. He would have a perfect right to speak to the woman he adores. It wouldn't sound so foolish then. I'll leave you to reach your own verdict. Your servant.

He leaves.

| MARTON: | Shall I ask the other steward to come up? |
| ARAMINTE: | Am I never to hear of anything but stewards? Go away, this is the wrong time to ask me questions. |

Marton leaves.

MME
ARGANTE: But she's right. Since he comes from the Comte, you
              simply must take him.

ARAMINTE: I don't want him.

COMTE: Is that because I proposed him?

ARAMINTE: You can draw your own conclusions, but I don't want
              him.

COMTE: You say this with an asperity I'm at a loss to
              understand.

MME
ARGANTE: Indeed, I hardly recognise you. What's made you
              angry?

ARAMINTE: Everything. The means have been scandalous, the
              behaviour offensive.

MME
ARGANTE: (Surprised) I don't understand you.

COMTE: Although I'm in no way responsible for what's
              happened, I see only too well that I'm included in your
              displeasure. I wouldn't wish to aggravate it by staying
              here any longer.

MME
ARGANTE: No, no, I'll come with you. I'll keep the Comte
              company until you come and join us. What are you
              thinking of, Araminte, I don't know what to make of
              you.

SCENE NINE

Araminte, Dubois.

DUBOIS: Well, you're rid of him at last. It doesn't matter what
              he does now, everyone's witnessed his folly. You
              needn't fear an outburst: he doesn't say a word. I've
              just seen him more dead than alive, sighing in a way
              that would make you laugh. I almost felt pity for him,
              He looked so undone, pale, miserable. I thought he
              might be ill.

ARAMINTE: *(Who's been distracted until now and hasn't looked at him. Suddenly, aloud.)* Someone must see to him. Was he followed at least? Why didn't you help him? Must that man be allowed to die?

DUBOIS: I called Arlequin, who won't leave his side. I doubt anything will happen, it's all over now. I just came to warn you that he might attempt to talk to you and I advise you not to. It's not worth your trouble.

ARAMINTE: *(Peevishly)* Stop meddling, this is my affair.

DUBOIS: That letter has freed you from any obligations towards him. It was I who advised Mademoiselle Marton to take it from Arlequin. Wasn't that clever of me?

ARAMINTE: *(Coldly)* So I have you to thank for the scene I've just been subjected to.

DUBOIS: *(Freely)* Yes.

ARAMINTE: Get out. I never want to see you again.

DUBOIS: *(As if in surprise.)* But I thought I'd done well.

ARAMINTE: Why didn't you obey me when I told you not to meddle any more? Instead, you put me into just the kind of embarrassing situation I wanted to avoid. Yes, and you're the one who started all those rumours about him. It wasn't your loyalty that made you tell me he loved me. It was for the pleasure of doing mischief. I pity that man for ever having had anything to do with you. He was your master, he looked after you, he was fond of you, and just recently he begged you on his knees to keep his secret. What do you do? You kill him, you betray me. You'll stop at nothing, I never want to see you again, and don't answer back.

DUBOIS: *(Laughing as he leaves.)* Nothing could be better.

SCENE TEN

Araminte, Marton.

MARTON: *(Sadly)* You dismissed me in such a way just now, I feel you no longer have much affection for me. I believe you'll be pleased to hear that I've come to ask if I may leave this house.

ARAMINTE: *(Cold)* Go, if you want to.

MARTON: Would you like me to leave today?

ARAMINTE: As you wish.

MARTON: These have been unhappy events for me.

ARAMINTE: Please, no explanations.

MARTON: I'm in despair.

ARAMINTE: *(With impatience.)* Are you unhappy about leaving? Then stay, I don't mind, but let's close the subject.

MARTON: You used to have such kindness for me. How can I stay any longer when you've become suspicious of me and no longer trust me?

ARAMINTE: What do you want me to trust you with? Am I to invent some secrets just to share them with you?

MARTON: You are sending me away. What have I done to incur your disfavour?

ARAMINTE: You're imagining it. You asked to leave and I said you could.

MARTON: Ah! Why did you allow me to act in a way that so displeased you? It was out of ignorance that I persecuted the most lovable man, a man who loves you more than anyone has ever loved before.

ARAMINTE: *(Aside)* Ah.

MARTON: And who's completely blameless. He's just spoken to me: I was his enemy, but I am no longer. He's told me everything: he'd never seen me before. It was Monsieur Remy who deceived me, not Dorante.

ARAMINTE: Good.

MARTON: How could you have been so cruel as to let me love a man who was never meant for me, who's worthy only of you? And now I'm suffering as much pain as I've caused him.

ARAMINTE: *(Gently)* Did you love him, Marton?

MARTON:	My feelings don't matter. It'll be more than enough if I have your friendship again.
ARAMINTE:	Ah, you have it, it's all yours.
MARTON:	*(Kissing her hand.)* I feel comforted now.
ARAMINTE:	No, Marton, not completely. You're crying. I feel sorry for you.
MARTON:	Don't take any notice. There's nothing so dear to me as your friendship.
ARAMINTE:	Go, now. There's Arlequin. I'll find a way to make you forget all your sorrows.

SCENE ELEVEN

Araminte, Marton, Arlequin.

ARAMINTE:	What do you want?
ARLEQUIN:	*(Sobbing)* I'm not sure I can tell you. My distress is so severe it's keeping me from talking. I've been betrayed by Mademoiselle Marton, she's behaved shamelessly, and with the utmost wickedness.
MARTON:	Forget the wickedness and tell us what you want.
ARLEQUIN:	That unfortunate letter! What a swindle!
ARAMINTE:	Tell us what you've come for.
ARLEQUIN:	Monsieur Dorante begs you on his knees to allow him to come and give you an account of some bits and pieces of paper that belong to you. He's waiting at the door. He's crying.
MARTON:	Tell him to come in.
ARLEQUIN:	*(To Araminte.)* Will you let him? I can't believe a word she says. Once I've been so vilely duped, I never again make the same mistake.
MARTON:	*(With a sad and moved air.)* Do speak to him. I'll leave you.
ARLEQUIN:	*(When Marton has left.)* You haven't answered me yet.
ARAMINTE:	He can come.

SCENE TWELVE

Dorante, Araminte.

ARAMINTE: Come in, Dorante.

DORANTE: I hardly dare appear before you.

ARAMINTE: *(Aside)* I'm not faring much better. *(Aloud)* You don't need to account for any papers; I trust you. It's not about that I have any complaints.

DORANTE: I have . . . something else to tell you . . . But I'm too embarrassed. I'm trembling and I can't speak.

ARAMINTE: *(Aside, with feeling.)* Ah! How I fear the end of all this.

DORANTE: *(Moved)* The tenant of one of your farms came . . .

ARAMINTE: *(Moved)* A tenant, yes, he could have . . .

DORANTE: Yes, he came. . . .

ARAMINTE: *(Still moved.)* I don't doubt it.

DORANTE: *(Still moved.)* I have some money for you.

ARAMINTE: Money, yes, we'll see. . . .

DORANTE: Whenever you choose to receive it.

ARAMINTE: I'll receive it . . . you'll give it to me. *(Aside)* I don't know what I'm saying.

DORANTE: Can you wait until this evening, or tomorrow?

ARAMINTE: Tomorrow! How can I keep you here until tomorrow?

DORANTE: *(With sorrow.)* I'm to spend the rest of my life far away from you. One day would mean so much.

ARAMINTE: I can't, Dorante. We must leave each other. Everyone knows that you love me, and they might think I don't mind.

DORANTE: I deserve some compassion.

ARAMINTE: Ah, Dorante, we all have our sorrows.

DORANTE: I've lost everything: I had a portrait, I no longer have it.

ARAMINTE: You don't need it, you know how to paint.

DORANTE: It will take a long time to make up for its loss – and
            this one would have been so dear to me: it's been in
            your hands.

ARAMINTE: You're being unreasonable.

DORANTE: Isn't it punishment enough that I must no longer see
            you? Please don't add to my pain.

ARAMINTE: Give you my portrait? Aren't you aware it would be to
            confess that I love you.

DORANTE: That you love me? Who could ever imagine that?

ARAMINTE: *(In an intense and naive tone.)* And yet, that's exactly
            what's happened.

DORANTE: *(Throwing himself at her knees.)* I'm dying.

ARAMINTE: I don't know what I'm doing any more. Dorante,
            please get up.

DORANTE: *(Getting up, tenderly.)* I don't deserve this happiness.
            It's overcome me and I don't deserve it. And I know
            you'll soon take it away from me, but it doesn't matter,
            I must tell you everything.

ARAMINTE: What do you mean?

DORANTE: Of all the events that have happened recently at your
            house, only two are genuine: one is my passion, which
            is infinite, and the other is the portrait I painted of
            you. Everything else has been engineered by a servant,
            who knew of my love for you and who took pity on me.
            He lured me with hope, and the irresistible prospect of
            seeing you more often. I consented to his plan. He
            believed he could show me off to advantage here.
            That's what my respect for you, my love, and my
            character will no longer allow me to conceal. I'd prefer
            to lose your love than owe it to the artifice that gained
            it for me. And I will suffer your hatred rather than the
            remorse of having deceived the one I adore.

ARAMINTE: *(Looking at him for a few moments without speaking.)* If
            anyone else had told me all this, I probably would hate
            you. But that you've confessed it yourself, and at such

a moment, changes everything. Your truthfulness is to
be marvelled at, it's disarmed me, and you've proved
yourself the most worthy man in the world. After all,
since you do love me, you cannot be blamed for
anything you did to win my heart. A lover is allowed to
have recourse to any means of pleasing at his disposal.
And when he's successful, he must be forgiven.

DORANTE: What? The enchanting Araminte finds excuses for my
conduct!

ARAMINTE: I see the Comte and my mother. Let me speak.

SCENE THIRTEEN

Dorante, Araminte, Comte, Madame Argante, Dubois, Arlequin.

MME
ARGANTE: *(As she sees Dorante.)* He's still here!

ARAMINTE: *(Coldly)* Yes, mother. *(To the Comte.)* There was talk of
marriage between us, Comte. It must no longer be
thought of. You deserve to be loved. My heart cannot
do you this justice. Nor is my rank suited to yours.

MME
ARGANTE: What now? What does this mean?

COMTE: I understand. And although I've said nothing to
Madame Argante, I had already decided to take my
leave of you. I've guessed everything: Dorante came
here because he loved you. He has succeeded in making
himself agreeable to you. It is he who's had the good
fortune to win you. That's all you had to tell me.

ARAMINTE: I have nothing to add, Comte.

MME
ARGANTE: *(Outraged)* To win a fortune! Him!

COMTE: *(Sadly)* There's only the matter of that dispute between
us, and we'll settle it amicably. I said I would not go to
court over it, and I'll keep my word.

ARAMINTE: You're very generous. It will be sufficient if you send
me someone who can settle it.

MME
ARGANTE: What a downfall! That accursed steward can be your
             husband as much as he pleases, he'll never be my son-
             in-law.

ARAMINTE: We'll let her anger pass.

             They leave.

DUBOIS: Ouf! I'm covered in glory. I believe I have the right to
             call that woman my daughter-in-law.

ARLEQUIN: We don't care about the painting any more. The
             original will provide us with enough copies.

                          THE END

SUCCESSFUL STRATEGIES

SUCCESSFUL STRATEGIES received its London première in this translation at the Lyric Theatre, Hammersmith in 1983. The cast was as follows:

DORANTE	Nick Dunning
BLAISE	John Price
ARLEQUIN	Sam Dale
LISETTE	Maggie Wells
LA COMTESSE	Holly Wilson
LA MARQUISE	Sandra Voe
FRONTIN	James Smith
LE CHEVALIER	Philip Voss
DIRECTOR	Mike Alfreds
SET, COSTUME AND LIGHTING	Paul Dart

CHARACTERS

DORANTE

BLAISE

ARLEQUIN

LISETTE

LA COMTESSE

LA MARQUISE

FRONTIN

LE CHEVALIER

ACT ONE

SCENE ONE

Dorante, Blaise.

DORANTE: Well, Master Blaise, what do you want? Speak, is there something I can do for you?

BLAISE: Oh, indeed, as it's the custom to say, you can very well.

DORANTE: What is it?

BLAISE: Ah, that's Monsieur Dorante all over, yes, that's him. When it's about being useful, he doesn't hesitate for a moment. What a pleasant way to be, a truly manly disposition.

DORANTE: I'd be delighted to help you.

BLAISE: Not at all, not at all, you're the one who delights others.

DORANTE: Tell me, then.

BLAISE: Put your hat on first.

DORANTE: No, I never do.

BLAISE: Good for you. I always wear my hat, that's not so bad either.

DORANTE: Well?

BLAISE: Well, what? How are you Monsieur Dorante? Still pink and plump? I knew the time when you were thin. But, by God, it's been well mended. You're in a good state of flesh.

DORANTE: I believe you had something to say to me. Do start, without any more compliments.

BLAISE: Oh, it was no more than a little touch of civility to start things off. As one ought to do.

DORANTE: I have some business to attend to.

BLAISE: That's too bad. But business won't perish from waiting.

DORANTE: I must leave you soon. Finish, please.

BLAISE: I'll begin then. I've come here because of my daughter,
           in that she's to be the wife of your valet Arlequin.

DORANTE: I know.

BLAISE: And I know you're willing because she's lady's maid to
           the Comtesse, who herself is to take you as her man.

DORANTE: So?

BLAISE: Because of all this, if it's agreeable to you, I've come to
           ask you for a favour.

DORANTE: What?

BLAISE: What it is, Monsieur Dorante, is that there will have to
           be the wedding clothes for Linette. And there will have
           to be a wedding as well, and what's worse, a great
           amount of eating for this wedding, and the foodstuff
           for this great eating, and ready money for this
           foodstuff. Everywhere ready money, except with us
           where there isn't any. And so, if through your
           approaches to the Comtesse, she could advance me
           some twenty-six francs on my wages for my
           gardening. . . .

DORANTE: I understand, Master Blaise, but I'd rather give you the
           money myself than ask the Comtesse for you. She
           wouldn't listen to any request of mine today. You think
           I'm about to marry her, you're mistaken. I believe I've
           been displaced by the Chevalier Damis. Go to him, and
           if you're not successful, I'll give you the money you
           need.

BLAISE: Now what I hear there astounds me so much, yes, I'm
           so stupefied, that I'm forgetting to thank you. A
           gentleman like you, with the features of a prince, with a
           heart big enough to offer me money, such a man to see
           himself abandoned by the very person of his mistress.
           It can't be. No, it can't be. She's our child, the
           Comtesse. It's our late-deceased wife who suckled her.
           Our wife was an upright woman, and it's upright milk
           she fed the Comtesse. Have no fear, put your mind
           back at ease, there isn't any Chevalier charging about in
           this business.

DORANTE: What I've told you is only too true, Master Blaise.

BLAISE: God's my witness, if I believed that, I'd be the man to
             show her the error of her ways. A Comtesse I saw a
             tiny babe! Would you like me to go and exhort her?

DORANTE: What will you tell her?

BLAISE: What I'll tell her! What I'll tell her! And what's this,
             I'll tell her, what's this. That's what I'll tell her,
             because I rocked that child in my arms, you hear, and
             that gives me rights.

DORANTE: Here's Arlequin, looking very sad.

<u>SCENE TWO</u>

ARLEQUIN: Ouf!

DORANTE: What's wrong?

ARLEQUIN: A deep sorrow for you and therefore a profound sorrow
             for me because a good servant always follows his
             master.

DORANTE: Well?

BLAISE: What's upsetting you?

ARLEQUIN: You must prepare yourself for grief. To all
             appearances, it will be overwhelming.

DORANTE: Tell me.

ARLEQUIN: I'm crying ahead of time so I can be consoled
             afterwards.

BLAISE: I'm beginning to feel sad myself.

DORANTE: Will you speak?

ARLEQUIN: Ah! I have nothing to say. I'm predicting your
             affliction.

DORANTE: I don't need your predictions!

BLAISE: Yes, who needs this bird of bad omen.

ARLEQUIN: It's just that not long ago, I was in the dining hall,
             where I was finishing off . . . but let's leave that aside.

DORANTE: I want to know everything.

ARLEQUIN: It was nothing . . . just a bottle of wine, which had
            been left and which I was finishing off, when I heard
            the Comtesse, coming in with the Chevalier.

DORANTE: And then?

ARLEQUIN: Since she might not have approved of my drinking in
            secret, I ran into the pantry with my bottle. First, I
            emptied it, to make it safe.

BLAISE: Yes, that's quite right.

DORANTE: Leave your bottle and tell me what concerns me.

ARLEQUIN: I'm speaking about the bottle because it was there. I
            didn't put it there.

BLAISE: You should leave it, if it's been drunk.

ARLEQUIN: So, there it is, empty. I put it on the floor.

DORANTE: Yes, yes.

ARLEQUIN: Then very quietly I looked through the keyhole.

DORANTE: And you saw the Comtesse with the Chevalier?

ARLEQUIN: Can you believe that stupid locksmith made the key
            hole so small I couldn't see through it?

BLAISE: That's too bad.

DORANTE: Then you're not sure it was the Comtesse?

ARLEQUIN: Yes I am, because my ears recognised her voice, and
            her voice wouldn't be there without her.

BLAISE: They couldn't avoid being together.

DORANTE: What were they saying?

ARLEQUIN: I can only remember the thoughts, I've forgotten the
            words.

DORANTE: Tell me the thoughts.

ARLEQUIN: To express the thoughts I need to know the words. But
            they were together and they were laughing
            uproariously. And that nasty Chevalier had his mouth
            wide open . . . you have to be in high spirits to laugh
            that much.

BLAISE: It's a sign of happiness, that's all.

ARLEQUIN: Yes, but that happiness doesn't bode well for us. When
               a man is that happy, that's good for him, but it's bad
               for another. And there's the other.

               Showing Dorante.

DORANTE: Leave me alone. Did you tell the Marquise I needed to
               speak to her?

ARLEQUIN: I can't remember if I told her, but I do remember I
               was supposed to tell her.

SCENE THREE

Arlequin, Blaise, Dorante, Lisette.

LISETTE: I don't know what your understanding is, but your
               calm surprises me. If you're not careful my mistress
               will slip away from you. I could be wrong, but I'm
               afraid for you.

DORANTE: I suspect as much myself, but what can I do?

BLAISE: Is it on the way to becoming definite, child?

LISETTE: Yes. The Chevalier doesn't leave her side. He amuses
               her, flatters her, speaks soft words to her. She smiles.
               In the end, her heart might become involved, if it
               hasn't already. That makes me uneasy, because I have a
               high opinion of you. And here's someone who's
               supposed to marry me and it'll be inconvenient for us if
               you don't become master of the house.

ARLEQUIN: We wouldn't want two households.

DORANTE: I don't see what can be done. The Comtesse avoids me.

BLAISE: That's a very bad sign.

ARLEQUIN: And what does the Chevalier's valet, that Frontin, say
               to you, Lisette?

LISETTE: Sweet nothings which I answer with rudeness.

BLAISE: That's right, daughter, always be rude and unpleasant
               to Frontin. Shake your head when he talks to you and

say: Go your way. Faithfulness, child, faithfulness,
leave all those other confusions to the Comtesse. Isn't
that right?

DORANTE: I'm dying!

BLAISE: You mustn't die, that spoils everything. Let's work out
some management of this.

LISETTE: I see the Comtesse. She's alone. Let me talk to her. I'll
find out what she has in mind and let you know.

DORANTE: I'll leave you.

BLAISE: Remember, sweet child, always rude and unpleasant.
Shake your head when Frontin talks to you.

LISETTE: Don't worry.

SCENE FOUR

Lisette, Comtesse.

COMTESSE: I was looking for you. Who was with you just now?

LISETTE: Dorante.

COMTESSE: He's the one I wanted to talk to you about. What does
he say?

LISETTE: He says he doesn't have much to be pleased with. He's
right. What do you think?

COMTESSE: He still loves me then?

LISETTE: Does he love you? You know very well he hasn't
changed. Don't you love him any more?

COMTESSE: What do you mean by any more? Did I ever love him?
I only Noticed him. And to Notice a man is not quite
to love him. It might lead to it, but it's not yet love.

LISETTE: I've heard you say he was the most amiable man in the
world.

COMTESSE: Perhaps.

LISETTE: I've seen you wait for him anxiously.

COMTESSE: I have an impatient nature.

LISETTE: You were upset when he didn't come.

COMTESSE: All that's true. As I said, I noticed him. I still notice him, but nothing commits me to him. And since he sometimes talks to you and you believe that he loves me, I'd like you to find a clever way of soothing him as far as I am concerned.

LISETTE: And all this for the Chevalier Damis, whose only distinguishing feature is that he comes from the South and you find that amusing. What a fickle heart you have. You have so much sense, how can you be unfaithful? Because that's what people will say.

COMTESSE: Well, call me unfaithful then. Do you think you frighten me with that big word? Unfaithful! These words are used to intimidate the faint-hearted. They're given weight but when you think about them, they're worthless.

LISETTE: What are you saying? You're so hardened on this subject! I never knew you were so lost: a heart that betrays its faith, that breaks its word!

COMTESSE: This heart, when it gives its word and breaks it, time and time again, is only following its call. It goes wherever its changing impulses carry it, and cannot do otherwise. What's all this nonsense? Far from calling unfaithfulness a crime, I maintain that, if tempted, one mustn't hesitate for an instant. Otherwise, you're deceiving people, and that must be avoided at all costs.

LISETTE: But, but . . . you've turned this in such a way I believe you must be right. Yes; unfaithfulness can sometimes become a duty. I would never have suspected it!

COMTESSE: You see how obvious it is.

LISETTE: So obvious I'm considering whether to be unfaithful myself.

COMTESSE: Dorante has charming notions. Am I, just because he loves me, never to dare cast a look elsewhere? Is he the only one who has a right to find me young and lovely? Must I seem a hundred years old to everyone else and bury all my attractions? Am I to devote my whole life to the sad sterility of pleasing only him?

LISETTE:	That's what he seems to expect.
COMTESSE:	Oh, no doubt. That's how these gentlemen want us to live. According to them, there must be only one man and he must compose your entire universe. All the others are debarred, they might as well be dead. Too bad if your self-regard isn't satisfied and you sometimes wish for these others. Faithfulness, stupid faithfulness has ordained that you must be content with only one captive. Resign yourself and bear with it. What oppression, Lisette, what oppression. Go, go and talk to Dorante, forget your reservations. Do you think men go to such lengths when they want to leave us? Doesn't every day bring new proof of their inconstancy? Do they have privileges we're not allowed to enjoy? You must be joking. The Chevalier loves me, I don't dislike him. I won't do any violence to my inclinations.
LISETTE:	Now that I'm so well-informed, let abandoned lovers seek sympathy where they will. I'm cured of the compassion I had for them.
COMTESSE:	It's not that I don't respect Dorante, but what one respects is often boring. He's coming back. I want to spare myself his lamentations. Use this moment to get rid of him.

SCENE FIVE

Dorante, Comtesse, Lisette, Arlequin.

DORANTE:	*(Stopping the Comtesse.)* Comtesse! I've just arrived and you run away?
COMTESSE:	Ah, it's you, Dorante. I'm not running away, I'm going back where I came from.
DORANTE:	Please, listen to me for a moment.
COMTESSE:	No more than a moment, I'm expecting company.
DORANTE:	They'll be announced, if they come. Allow me to speak of my love.
COMTESSE:	Is that all? I know your love by heart. What does this love want with me now?

DORANTE: Ah, Comtesse, I see I'm boring you.

COMTESSE: To tell you the truth, your prologue isn't entertaining.

DORANTE: I'm so unhappy! You've changed so much towards me. You're making me lose all hope.

COMTESSE: Dorante, how long is this dirge going to last?

DORANTE: And I still love you, despite such cruel answers!

COMTESSE: Cruel answers! With what relish you say that. You would have made a wonderful hero of romance, Dorante, your heart missed its vocation.

DORANTE: How callous you are.

COMTESSE: (*Laughing*) That mode of address won't reform me.

ARLEQUIN: (*In back, whining.*) Hi! Hi! Hi!

COMTESSE: See, your miseries are so contagious they've contaminated your valet.

ARLEQUIN: I'm affected by my master's misfortune.

DORANTE: Only my respect for you is making me contain my anger.

COMTESSE: Anger? How's that? May I ask what you have to complain about? Is it the love you feel for me? I can do nothing about it. It's not a crime to seem lovable to you. Is it then the love I don't feel for you? It's not my fault if it isn't there. You have the right to wish that I loved you, but to blame me because I don't is unreasonable. Your feelings do not dictate mine. Beware: I'm not in your debt. You may sigh as much as you please, I can't stop you, but don't ask me to sigh with you. I don't even have to find your sighs entertaining. I used to think them bearable, but the tone they've taken today bores me. I suggest you behave accordingly. Goodbye.

DORANTE: One last word: you do not love me any more?

COMTESSE: Any more? I can't quite recollect ever having loved you.

DORANTE: No! And I swear I won't recollect it either as long as I live.

COMTESSE: In that case, you'll be forgetting no more than a dream.

    She leaves.

SCENE SIX

Dorante, Arlequin, Lisette.

DORANTE: *(Stopping Lisette.)* The traitress! Wait, Lisette.

ARLEQUIN: That's not a very edifying little heart the Comtesse has there.

DORANTE: *(To Lisette.)* You spoke to her about me. I know only too well what she thinks. What did she say specifically?

LISETTE: I don't have time: my mistress is expecting company, she may need me.

ARLEQUIN: Oh! Oh! Listen to that.

DORANTE: Lisette, are you abandoning me? What reasons does she give for her behaviour?

LISETTE: Very good ones, I must admit. Faithfulness is useless, it's wrong to have any. It's no good having lovely eyes, only one man gains by that, all the others are dead. One mustn't deceive anyone: then one is buried and self-regard doesn't have its share, it's as if one were a hundred years old. You're respected, but boredom has come into it. One might as well be an old woman, and that works against you.

DORANTE: What's the meaning of this strange speech?

ARLEQUIN: I've never seen such ugly words.

DORANTE: Explain yourself.

LISETTE: What? You don't understand? Well, you're Noticed.

DORANTE: Do you mean that I'm loved?

LISETTE: No, it might lead to it, but it's not yet love.

DORANTE: I don't follow. Is the Chevalier loved?

LISETTE: He's a most amiable man.

DORANTE: What about me?

LISETTE: You were most amiable. Do you understand me now?

DORANTE: I'm mortified!

ARLEQUIN: And what about me, little maid of my soul, what do you make of me?

LISETTE: You? I Notice you.

ARLEQUIN: And I curse you, chambermaid of the devil.

SCENE SEVEN

Arlequin, Dorante, Marquise (arriving).

ARLEQUIN: What delightful people we're dealing with.

DORANTE: My heart's frozen.

ARLEQUIN: My breath's shortened.

MARQUISE: You seem very unhappy, Dorante.

DORANTE: I'm betrayed, Marquise, assassinated, the knife's being twisted in my breast.

ARLEQUIN: I'm smothered, Marquise, I'm strangled, I'm Noticed!

MARQUISE: I suppose this has something to do with the Comtesse?

DORANTE: Yes.

MARQUISE: Could I have a word with you?

DORANTE: Indeed. I want to talk to you.

MARQUISE: Tell your valet to warn us if anyone is coming.

DORANTE: Go and watch for us.

ARLEQUIN: Heaven console us. We're all three on the street. You're there too, Marquise, your Chevalier isn't worth any more than our Comtesse and Lisette: we're three hearts out of work.

MARQUISE: Leave us.

            Arlequin leaves.

SCENE EIGHT

Marquise, Dorante.

MARQUISE: Have we both been abandoned, Dorante?

DORANTE: As you see, Marquise.

MARQUISE: And you can't think of anything to do about it?

DORANTE: I no longer know what to try. We're being abandoned
            in such a definite manner. We were badly matched,
            Marquise, why aren't you the one I love?

MARQUISE: Well, Dorante, try to love me.

DORANTE: If only I could!

MARQUISE: that's not a flattering answer, but I expected nothing
            more from your condition.

DORANTE: I'm so sorry, I don't know what I'm saying. I'm
            distracted.

MARQUISE: Don't bother to excuse yourself.

DORANTE: You're lovely, it's not difficult to see that, and I've
            regretted so many times that I didn't pay more
            attention to you. I've told myself so many times. . . .

MARQUISE: The more compliments you try, the more insulting you
            are. There's no sweetness in your words. Let's change
            the subject.

DORANTE: You're my last resort. You're right. I must love you:
            it's the only way to punish the traitress I adore.

MARQUISE: I know an easier way to revenge ourselves. I want to
            punish the Comtesse, but I also want to give her back
            to you. And I will give her back to you.

DORANTE: The Comtesse would come back to me!

MARQUISE: More loving than ever.

DORANTE: Is that possible?

MARQUISE: And it won't even cost you the effort of loving me.

DORANTE: As you wish.

MARQUISE: Wait: I can allow you not to love me only if you
            pretend to do so.

DORANTE: Easily, I'll do anything you like.

MARQUISE: Did she love you very much?

DORANTE: I thought so.

MARQUISE: And she was convinced that you loved her?

DORANTE: I adore her and she knows it.

MARQUISE: Good. As long as she's certain.

DORANTE: What about the Chevalier who left you for her? Do we
            allow him time to make himself loved by the Comtesse?

MARQUISE: If the Comtesse believes she loves him, she's mistaken.
            She only wanted to take him away from me. And if she
            believes she no longer loves you, she's also mistaken. It
            is only her vanity that neglects you.

DORANTE: That could be.

MARQUISE: I know my own sex, you must let me handle this. What
            we'll do is . . . someone's coming. I'll talk to you later.

SCENE NINE

Arlequin, Dorante, Marquise.

ARLEQUIN: *(As he comes.)* Ah! I'm in such pain!

DORANTE: Have you disturbed us just to moan? You're
            disgraceful.

ARLEQUIN: I've come with the best grace in the world to tell you
            there's a rogue out there who's asking for the
            Marquise. Shall I ask him to come in, or shall I give
            him a beating?

MARQUISE: Who is he?

ARLEQUIN: A scoundrel who stole my Lisette and who's called
            Frontin.

MARQUISE: The Chevalier's valet? Let him come, I want to speak
            to him.

ARLEQUIN: That's a nasty acquaintance you have there!

He leaves.

SCENE TEN

Marquise, Dorante.

MARQUISE: For all that he's a valet, Frontin is an able lad and I've asked him to spy on the Chevalier and the Comtesse. We'll listen to what he has to say and make sure they do love each other. If you don't have the strength to look unconcerned, you had better leave.

DORANTE: I'm mortified, but have no fears.

SCENE ELEVEN

Marquise, Dorante, Arlequin, Frontin.

ARLEQUIN: *(Bringing in Frontin.)* Come, Master Rogue, come in.

FRONTIN: I'll give you my answer on my way out.

ARLEQUIN: *(Leaving)* The one I'm preparing for you has no words.

MARQUISE: Come here, Frontin.

SCENE TWELVE

Marquise, Frontin, Dorante.

MARQUISE: What do you have to tell me?

FRONTIN: Can I speak freely?

MARQUISE: Absolutely.

DORANTE: Who's concerned in this?

MARQUISE: The Comtesse and the Chevalier. Stay, it'll amuse you.

DORANTE: Willingly.

FRONTIN: It might even give you something to think about.

DORANTE: Let's see.

FRONTIN: As soon as I had promised you I would watch what
             was taking place between my master and the Comtesse,
             I began to lie in ambush . . .

MARQUISE: Try to be brief.

FRONTIN: When I'm brief I never reach the end.

MARQUISE: Does the Chevalier still love me?

FRONTIN: There's no trace of it. He doesn't know who you are.

MARQUISE: And so he must love the Comtesse?

FRONTIN: Does he love her! You're merely scratching the surface.
             You might as well call a roaring forest fire a spark. His
             heart burns, he's consumed with love.

DORANTE: (With a cheerful air.) And the Comtesse does not dislike
             him, it seems.

FRONTIN: The truth is more than a thousand miles from that.

DORANTE: I'm to understand she returns his love.

FRONTIN: Nonsense! She no longer returns anything. She's
             already returned all there is to return. Or rather, in this
             business, there was no time to offer or to return
             anything. Imagine two hearts that run off together at a
             speed never seen before. No one knows who let out the
             first sigh, it was always a duet.

DORANTE: (Laughing) Ah! Ah! Ah! (Aside) I'm dying.

MARQUISE: (Aside) Take care . . . (To Frontin.) do you have proof of
             this?

FRONTIN: Let me bring forward the most trustworthy witnesses:
             my eyes, my ears . . . Yesterday, the Comtesse . . .

DORANTE: That's enough. They love each other, the episode is
             closed. What more can he say?

MARQUISE: Finish.

FRONTIN: Yesterday, the Comtesse and my master were taking a
             walk in the garden. I follow them. They go into the
             woods, I go into the woods. They take a path, I slip

into the thicket. They talk, but I only hear
unintelligible voices. I slide, I slither, and from shrub
to shrub I eventually find myself in a position to hear
and even see them through the leaves . . . Ah! What a
beautiful sight, cried the Chevalier. What a beautiful
sight! He held in one hand a miniature and in the other
the Comtesse's hand. What a beautiful sight! He's a
Southerner, you understand, and I'm telling you this as
a Southerner would, even though I'm from the North –
one can do anything when one is precise and diligent.

MARQUISE: Very good.

DORANTE: (Aside) Very bad.

FRONTIN: Now, this portrait, of which I could make out the chin
and a small part of the ear, was of the Comtesse. Yes,
she was saying, they say it is a good likeness. As good
as it can be, said my master, as good as it can be, but
without those thousand charms of yours that I so
adore, charms which a painter might observe, but
cannot hope to reproduce. No, they belong exclusively
to nature's paintbrush. Come, come, you're flattering
me, cried the Comtesse, her eyes sparkling with vanity,
you're flattering me. No, Comtesse, let me choke if I
do. I debase you by even daring to talk of your charms.
Words cannot begin to touch upon them; no, your
likeness is to be found only in my heart. Are there not
two of us there, the Marquise and myself, answered the
Comtesse. The Marquise! And where would she find
room? You would fill a thousand hearts, if I had them.
My love no longer knows where to put itself, it's over-
flowing, it must cascade into my words, my feelings,
my thoughts. It spreads everywhere, my soul is
bursting its banks. And so speaking, he sometimes
kissed the hand of the Comtesse, and sometimes the
portrait. And if she withdrew her hand, he threw
himself on to the portrait, and when she asked for the
portrait, he took back the hand. So the movement, as
you see, went like this and like that. It was a sight to
behold.

DORANTE: What a tale, Marquise.

The Marquise motions Dorante to keep quiet.

FRONTIN: What were you saying?

DORANTE: I was telling the Marquise how amusing I find this.

FRONTIN: I should hope so. To continue: Give me back my
              portrait, Chevalier, give it back . . . But, Comtesse . . .
              But, Chevalier . . . But, Comtesse, if I'm to give back
              the copy, I must have the original as compensation.
              Oh, no, not that . . . Oh yes, just that . . . The
              Chevalier falls to his knees: Comtesse, in the name of
              your innumerable graces, give me the copy as security,
              while I wait for the person. Accord this refreshment to
              my ardour . . . But Chevalier, to give away one's
              portrait is to give away one's heart . . . I could endure
              having them both . . . But . . . There is no but, my life
              is yours, the portrait is mine, let each keep what
              belongs to him. . . . Well, you're the one who's keeping
              the portrait, I'm not the one who's giving it to you . . .
              A deal: I'll accept the responsibility. It's I who have
              taken it, and you have done no more than allow me to
              take it . . . You're taking advantage of my kindness.
              Ah! Here it's the Comtesse who sighs, Ah! Delight of
              my soul. That's the Chevalier, letting out the second
              sigh.

DORANTE: Ah! . . . .

FRONTIN: And it's you who've provided the third.

DORANTE: Yes, those sighs are so amusing I'm imitating them.
              You too, Marquise, must imitate.

MARQUISE: I'm imagining them. (She laughs.) Ha! Ha! Ha!

FRONTIN: This morning, in the gallery. . . .

DORANTE: (To the Marquise.) Stop him!

MARQUISE: That's enough, Frontin.

FRONTIN: But the fragments I have left are exquisite.

MARQUISE: I know enough.

FRONTIN: Is our agreement to be continued on the same terms?

MARQUISE: There's no need.

FRONTIN: (To Dorante.) Perhaps you'd like to become my patron?

DORANTE: No.

FRONTIN: That no, if I know my business, brooks no reply and I
              need do no more than bow myself off.

    He leaves.

SCENE THIRTEEN

Marquise, Dorante.

MARQUISE: We can no longer doubt their secret understanding, but
              if you continue to play your part so badly, we'll lose
              everything.

DORANTE: I confess his tale gave me pain. I'll control myself
              better next time. Ah, the traitress, she never gave me
              her portrait.

SCENE FOURTEEN

Arlequin, Marquise, Dorante.

ARLEQUIN: The other robber's coming.

DORANTE: Who?

ARLEQUIN: The master of the one who just left.

DORANTE: Go.

    He leaves.

SCENE FIFTEEN

Marquise, Dorante.

MARQUISE: We haven't had time to talk through our plan, but
              remember that you love me, that this must be believed,
              that your rival's here, and that you must appear
              indifferent. I don't have time to say more.

DORANTE: Trust me, I'll play my part well.

SCENE SIXTEEN

Dorante, Chevalier.

CHEVALIER: Dorante, I wanted to talk to you.

DORANTE: Willingly, Chevalier, but hurry. The post is coming and I want to send off a packet.

CHEVALIER: I'll finish in a flash. I'm your friend, and I've come to ask you to free me of a qualm.

DORANTE: You?

CHEVALIER: Yes, relieve my honour of a little quibble. Tell me, is it right, is it wrong? They say you love the Comtesse. I don't believe it. And it's between the yes and the no to that question that lies the little case of conscience I bring you.

DORANTE: I understand: you would like me no longer to love the Comtesse.

CHEVALIER: The delicacy of my feelings requires your indifference. I love her.

DORANTE: Is she disposed in your favour?

CHEVALIER: I don't need any favours. She does me justice.

DORANTE: You mean she likes you.

CHEVALIER: When I said I loved her, I said everything. Spare my modesty.

DORANTE: I can't talk to your modesty; it's Southern. Let's speak plainly: does she love you?

CHEVALIER: Yes, I say. Her eyes have already broached that subject; they solicit an answer from my heart. Shall I put 'approved' at the bottom of the request? I'm waiting for your consent.

DORANTE: You have it, but you must give me a fair exchange.

CHEVALIER: What?

DORANTE: There are beautiful eyes you once knew, which now solicit my heart.

CHEVALIER: The beautiful eyes of the Marquise?

DORANTE: Yes.

CHEVALIER: And you've been restrained by the interest you suspected I took in them?

DORANTE: I have.

CHEVALIER: I emancipate you.

DORANTE: I warn you I'll marry her.

CHEVALIER: We'll have a cavalcade of weddings.

DORANTE: You'll marry the Comtesse?

CHEVALIER: The hopes of my posterity depend on it.

DORANTE: Soon?

CHEVALIER: Tomorrow will perhaps herald the termination of our celibacy.

DORANTE: *(Embarrassed)* Goodbye. I'm delighted.

CHEVALIER: *(Putting out his hand.)* Your hand. Are you fond of me?

DORANTE: Ah, yes. . . .

CHEVALIER: My fondness for you is immeasurable. I'm your friend for a century and after that, we'll renew our lease. I'm your servant.

DORANTE: Yes, yes, tomorrow.

CHEVALIER: What do you mean by tomorrow? I'm your servant for all time past, time present, time future. And you're the same for me, it seems.

DORANTE: So it seems. Goodbye.

He leaves.

SCENE SEVENTEEN

Chevalier, Frontin.

FRONTIN: I was waiting for him to leave.

CHEVALIER: What do you want? I'm anxious to meet with my Comtesse.

FRONTIN: Wait! This is serious. I made my report to the Marquise.

CHEVALIER: So? You told her that I love the Comtesse and that the Comtesse loves me. What does she say? Tell me quickly.

FRONTIN: She says you're doing a good thing.

CHEVALIER: I'll continue to do a good thing. Goodbye.

FRONTIN: You mustn't dream of it! Go immediately to the Marquise, rekindle her love. If not, you're a dead man, buried, obliterated forever from her memory.

CHEVALIER: *(Laughing)* Heh! Heh! Heh!

FRONTIN: I don't think it's funny.

CHEVALIER: What do I care about being obliterated? I die in one memory, I come to life again in another. Do I not have the memory of the Comtesse in which to live?

FRONTIN: Yes, but in that memory, I'm afraid, one fine day you'll succumb to sudden death. Dorante died that way, from a fit of caprice.

CHEVALIER: No, the caprice that killed Dorante stands here. I dispatched him, as I've dispatched so many others before. Don't worry, Frontin: the Comtesse has received me into her heart, she'll have to keep me there.

FRONTIN: I fear she has the kind of heart in which one might set up camp, but must never hope to settle.

CHEVALIER: That's a love to my taste. Trust to my good fortune. When you know me better, you'll be less wary.

FRONTIN: I've trusted to fortune before, it didn't do me any good. Here's Lisette, you should dispose her mistress in my favour.

SCENE EIGHTEEN

Lisette, Frontin, Chevalier.

LISETTE: My mistress is asking for you.

CHEVALIER: I'm running to her, Lisette. Please put some sense back into this fool. You've taken his brains away, he argues that he loves you.

LISETTE: Why doesn't he confide in me?

FRONTIN: Well, my charmer, I love you. Now you're as well informed as I am.

LISETTE: Well, my lad, don't despair. Now you're better informed than you were. I'll go and tell my mistress that you're coming.

FRONTIN: Goodbye, my enchantress.

SCENE NINETEEN

Frontin, Chevalier.

FRONTIN: You're right. Events look favourable. The Comtesse loves you. You're a Southerner, I'm a Northerner. Both are indeed titles to fortune.

CHEVALIER: I'll be the guarantor of yours.

FRONTIN: *(Aside)* If I had a choice in the matter, I'd look for one elsewhere.

END OF ACT ONE

ACT TWO

SCENE ONE

Dorante, Arlequin.

DORANTE: I want to have a word with you.

ARLEQUIN: A dozen, if you like.

DORANTE: Arlequin, I see you running after Lisette all the time.

ARLEQUIN: If I want to catch her, I have to run after her: she's always running away.

DORANTE: Do you prefer serving me to serving anyone else?

ARLEQUIN: Of course. The only person I prefer serving is myself. That's normal: first me, then you, that's how it's arranged in my mind. The rest of the world can look after itself.

DORANTE: If you prefer me to anyone else, you'll have to resign yourself on the subject of Lisette.

ARLEQUIN: That subject doesn't concern you. It's love I feel for her, and it's not love you need from me. You wouldn't know what to do with it.

DORANTE: True, but I forbid you ever to speak of love to Lisette. I even want you to avoid her, to break off with her.

ARLEQUIN: But what you want bears no resemblance to what I want. Why can't we agree today as we did yesterday?

DORANTE: Things have changed. The Comtesse might suspect me of using you to find out from Lisette what she's doing. So, leave Lisette alone. I'll reward you for your sacrifice.

ARLEQUIN: But I'll die of the sacrifice long before I can enjoy the reward.

DORANTE: No more arguments. Marton is lady's maid to the Marquise and she's well worth your Lisette.

ARLEQUIN: If the Marquise herself were thrown in, I'd still be cheated.

DORANTE: Choose. Do you prefer your dismissal or Marton?

ARLEQUIN: I can't say, I've experienced neither one nor the other.

DORANTE: You'll experience your dismissal today if you don't follow my orders. If you do, Lisette will miss you.

ARLEQUIN: She'll miss me! Why didn't you say that before?

DORANTE: Go, I see the Marquise.

ARLEQUIN: I'll obey your orders, but only if I'm to be missed.

DORANTE: By the way, keep this quiet. Since I'd already consented to your marriage, it would shock the Comtesse to learn I'm opposing it now. All I can allow you to say is that you prefer Marton, who's being offered to you by the Marquise.

ARLEQUIN: Have no fears, the only people acting dishonourably will be the Marquise and myself. She's giving me Marton. I'm accepting her. You're only allowing it to happen.

DORANTE: Excellent. Go, then.

ARLEQUIN: *(Coming back.)* But I'll be missed?

        He leaves.

SCENE TWO

Marquise, Dorante.

MARQUISE: Have you instructed your valet?

DORANTE: Yes.

MARQUISE: That little touch could be useful. If the Comtesse hears of it, she'll feel the sting.

DORANTE: I'm beginning to believe we'll succeed. She's already startled by my behaviour towards her. She, who is always expecting recriminations, almost asked me why I wasn't making any.

MARQUISE: If you stand firm, you'll see her cry with pain.

DORANTE: I'll wait for the tears.

MARQUISE: I guarantee nothing, if you don't go that far.

DORANTE: And how is your Chevalier behaving?

MARQUISE: Don't mention him. We'll bring about his downfall and
               let him become what he will. I'm expecting the
               Comtesse. She mustn't see us together, it might seem
               obvious.

DORANTE: I have a little plan, which I'll put into effect after you've
               left her.

MARQUISE: Don't spoil anything.

DORANTE: Trust me.

                              He leaves.

SCENE THREE

Marquise, Comtesse.

COMTESSE: Since you've asked to see me alone, Marquise, it must
               be a serious matter.

MARQUISE: I only have one question, Comtesse. And since you are,
               by nature, truthful, since you are sincerity itself,
               frankness incarnate, our conversation will not be a long
               one.

COMTESSE: I understand: you do not think me very sincere, but your
               compliments exhort me to be so.

MARQUISE: More or less. Will you?

COMTESSE: To show you my willingness, I'll begin by telling you
               that I don't know.

MARQUISE: If I asked, 'Does the Chevalier love you?' would you
               tell me?

COMTESSE: No, Marquise. I don't want to quarrel with you, and
               you'd hate me if I told you the truth.

MARQUISE: I give you my word that I won't.

COMTESSE: You'll break it. And I wouldn't blame you. There exist
               emotions more powerful than we are.

MARQUISE: Why would I hate you?

COMTESSE: Has it not been said that the Chevalier loved you?

MARQUISE: It was said correctly.

COMTESSE: Just so. Perhaps you believed it yourself?

MARQUISE: I confess I did.

COMTESSE: And I'm to tell you that he loves me! You wouldn't advise that.

MARQUISE: Is that all? I'd like to be rid of him. I hope from the bottom of my heart that he loves you.

COMTESSE: In that case, you can thank Heaven. Your hopes have been realised.

MARQUISE: I'm delighted.

COMTESSE: You've put me at ease. Not that I condone his behaviour. You're so lovely he ought never to have looked at anyone else. Is it possible he was less smitten than was generally believed?

MARQUISE: No, he was very smitten, but I can excuse him. If I am lovely, you are even more so. And no one knows better than you how to make yourself lovely.

COMTESSE: How to make myself lovely . . . Ah, you're not that delighted, Marquise. Your compliments are deteriorating. I'll make do with this one, it has a touch of spite which is not without merit: Jealousy is praise.

MARQUISE: Jealous? Me?

COMTESSE: Could a compliment that accuses me of being a coquette have any other source, Marquise?

MARQUISE: It never occurred to me to call you a coquette.

COMTESSE: These things are said before one has even thought of them.

MARQUISE: Are you not, in all honesty, a little coquettish?

COMTESSE: Indeed. But why stop at a little? Don't deny yourself the pleasure of saying that I'm more than a little. It doesn't prevent you from being as much of a coquette as I am.

MARQUISE: I don't give such a good demonstration of it.

COMTESSE: It's only demonstrated when one succeeds. Lack of
             success has allowed many a coquette to escape
             unnoticed. One retires quietly, a little humiliated, but
             unobserved. That's the advantage of failure.

MARQUISE: I'll succeed when I choose, it's not as difficult as you
             imply. The Chevalier might not be with you, had I not
             found his heart so untempting.

COMTESSE: I won't argue with that contempt. But when pride
             wishes to save face, that's how it speaks.

MARQUISE: Shall we wager that these events won't wound my pride
             if I don't want them to.

COMTESSE: Are you hoping to win back the Chevalier? If you can,
             I'll hand him over.

MARQUISE: Presumably you love him?

COMTESSE: Well enough, but I'll love him even more, so that he'll
             resist you better. One needs all of one's weapons with
             you.

MARQUISE: Have no fears. I'll leave him to you. Goodbye.

COMTESSE: Why? Let's agree to fight over him, but to forgive
             whoever wins. I'll only enter the struggle on those
             terms. I don't want you to reproach me.

MARQUISE: Are you so certain you'll win?

COMTESSE: I'll play a better game than you.

MARQUISE: I was playing a good game when you took him away. I
             could win him back.

COMTESSE: Try to play the winning hand.

MARQUISE: I may already have it.

COMTESSE: May one ask how?

MARQUISE: Dorante is not a losing hand, Comtesse. Goodbye.

             She leaves.

SCENE FOUR

Comtesse (alone).

COMTESSE: Dorante! She wants to take Dorante away from me!
            That woman's losing her mind, she's become distracted
            with jealousy. Poor thing!

SCENE FIVE

Dorante, Comtesse.

DORANTE: *(Arriving very quickly and pretending to take the
            Comtesse for the Marquise.)* Well, Marquise, what
            qualms can you have now? *(Seeing the Comtesse.)* Ah,
            Comtesse, I'm so sorry, I thought you were the
            Marquise. I thought I saw her here a moment ago and
            I was so preoccupied I took you for her.

COMTESSE: There's no harm done, Dorante, but what are these
            qualms? What do they mean?

DORANTE: It was just the continuation of a conversation we were
            having.

COMTESSE: But in this conversation, what were these qualms
            about? I want you to tell me.

DORANTE: It was a trifling matter. I can't remember very well
            myself. I believe she was curious to know how I stood
            in your heart.

COMTESSE: I assume you had the discretion not to tell her.

DORANTE: I wouldn't make the mistake of boasting in vain.

COMTESSE: No, you might make the mistake of telling the truth.
            What did she want with that information?

DORANTE: Mere curiosity, as I said. . . .

COMTESSE: But this curiosity led to qualms. I don't understand.

DORANTE: I used that word accidentally, I don't know why.

COMTESSE: Accidentally. For an intelligent man, you're getting out of this rather badly, Dorante. There's some mystery here.

DORANTE: It seems I can't convince you there isn't. Let's talk of something else. Speaking of curiosity, has it been long since you received letters from Paris? The Marquise expects some. She loves to keep in touch with what's going on, and I'm certain her friends won't deny her.

COMTESSE: I pity your embarrassment.

DORANTE: Are you coming back to that trifle?

COMTESSE: I thought I had more power over you.

DORANTE: You will always have power over me, Comtesse. It isn't my fault if the power you once had has decreased a little. I'll leave you so as not to succumb to what is still left you.

He leaves.

COMTESSE: I don't recognise Dorante in that manner.

SCENE SIX

Comtesse (deep in thought), Chevalier.

CHEVALIER: It seems my Comtesse has fallen into a deep state of meditation.

COMTESSE: The affliction of Dorante and the Marquise disturbs me. We were talking of marriage, Chevalier, we must delay it.

CHEVALIER: Delay it!

COMTESSE: For about a fortnight.

CHEVALIER: That's more than a century. Why this delay?

COMTESSE: Haven't you seen how agitated they are?

CHEVALIER: What do I need to see anything for?

COMTESSE: These people are already devastated. Do you want to push them over the edge? We're not in such a hurry.

CHEVALIER: We are in a hurry: I'm dying. If the case needs a victim, why choose me?

COMTESSE: Let's be frank: our association has a slight air of infidelity. They might once have believed that we loved them, we must be careful with them. I don't like to hurt anyone. You don't either, do you? You're not hard-hearted? They're your friends, as well as mine. Let's allow them to get used to the idea of our marriage.

CHEVALIER: For them to get used to it, I must live, and I defy you to keep me alive that long. Let's try to get them used to it at less expense to ourselves. Dying for the comfort of one's friends isn't yet in fashion. And then, what does it matter what they say now? Apparently, they're coming to an arrangement.

COMTESSE: An arrangement? What kind of an arrangement are you talking about?

CHEVALIER: I mean their hearts are making do.

COMTESSE: You have such a strange turn of phrase sometimes that I don't understand a word you say. Do you mean they love each other? Can't you talk like everyone else?

CHEVALIER: *(In a low voice.)* Love is not yet mentioned. Rather, they feel a gentle pleasure in seeing one another.

COMTESSE: A pleasure in seeing one another! Where did that notion come from? If you can prove to me that these people love each other, that they feel pleasure in seeing one another, if you can prove that, I'll marry you tomorrow, I'll marry you tonight! You see what importance I attach to this proof.

CHEVALIER: I can't put up the bond for their love.

COMTESSE: Prove only that they're consoling each other.

CHEVALIER: In that case, would you proceed?

COMTESSE: Yes, if I were certain they were at peace. But who can tell us that?

CHEVALIER: I have you there. The Marquise has asked Frontin to watch us and report on the state of our hearts.

COMTESSE: That already weakens your case. If they were forgetting
              us, they wouldn't bother with us.

CHEVALIER: Frontin may have already talked to them. Let his
              report govern us.

COMTESSE: Very well.

SCENE SEVEN

Chevalier, Frontin, Comtesse.

CHEVALIER: Frontin, have you seen the Marquise?

FRONTIN: Yes, and what's more, she was with Dorante. I've just
              left them.

CHEVALIER: Describe their behaviour. The Comtesse, out of the
              kindness of her heart, is afraid of driving them to
              despair. I say they're consoling each other. What's
              between them? Only this kindness is making her
              hesitate, do you understand?

FRONTIN: Perfectly. The Comtesse may marry you without
              uneasiness. Of despair, there's not a trace.

CHEVALIER: It's settled. Tonight you're mine.

COMTESSE: That's not so certain. Frontin doesn't seem to have
              observed carefully.

FRONTIN: I must object: despair is easy to recognise. Were it a
              little agitation, all fragile and discreet, it might pass
              unnoticed. But despair is large, it takes up room.
              People in despair move about restlessly. They wriggle,
              they writhe, they throw their arms about in big
              gestures and make noise. There's nothing of that.

CHEVALIER: He's telling the truth. I said to Dorante just now, I
              love the Comtesse, I have a passion for her. Well, keep
              her, he said peacefully.

COMTESSE: You're his rival. Do you expect him to confess his pain
              to you?

CHEVALIER: He was laughing, and his heart was at peace.

COMTESSE: The heart of a man who loved me with the most ardent
            passion that ever existed, at peace!

CHEVALIER: Barring mine.

COMTESSE: Yes, but let me say, by the way, I believe his heart is
            more loving than yours. It's not your fault: people love
            as they can and no one loved more than he. That's why
            I feel sorry for him. What makes Frontin say he's at
            peace? Aren't you paid by the Marquise and possibly by
            Dorante to watch us? Does one pay spies to observe
            what is no longer of interest?

FRONTIN: I'm badly paid. The Marquise is in arrears.

COMTESSE: And because she's ungenerous, you call her indifferent?

FRONTIN: Dorante still owes me wages.

COMTESSE: Leave your wages for a moment. What have you seen?
            What do you know?

CHEVALIER: (Low to Frontin.) Moderate your tale.

FRONTIN: Well, Frontin, they asked just now, do they love each
            other a little? Oh, a lot, I said. To cut it short:
            extremely.

COMTESSE: And. . . ?

FRONTIN: Not a sound. The Marquise hears me with a yawn and
            Dorante opens his snuff box, nonchalantly. I can get
            nothing more out of them.

COMTESSE: Leave us, Frontin, you're inept. Your valet's
            observations are laughable. He only saw the surface of
            things: it can't be as he said.

FRONTIN: I'll go the stake for it. Shall I tell you more? They love
            each other. They themselves told me to tell you this.

COMTESSE: (Laughing) Why didn't you begin with that, you idiot?
            You see how it is, Chevalier, they're consoling each
            other so enthusiastically to make us jealous. And their
            ineptitude shows the extent of their distress. Didn't I
            tell you so?

CHEVALIER: Passion is beginning to reveal itself, I confess.

COMTESSE: In a most grotesque way.

FRONTIN: Now, I understand! They want to hurt you. That's why Dorante, when he looked at his watch, didn't seem to see it, and he made a kind of face.

COMTESSE: Because his heart was not at peace.

CHEVALIER: That face is significant.

FRONTIN: And when he opened his snuff box, his fingers were trembling. His mouth was laughing, but without much gaiety, and the rest of the face didn't follow. It was doing something else.

COMTESSE: Because his heart was not laughing.

CHEVALIER: I surrender. Dorante sighs, he casts unsteady looks and my wedding moves back. To hell with this blockhead who's thrown my Comtesse into a state of compassion that could have tragic consequences for my happiness.

COMTESSE: Not at all: Dorante has behaved too shabbily to deserve consideration. There's the Marquise. I know her: she's coming in her usual sly manner to insinuate she and Dorante love each other. Let's hear it.

SCENE EIGHT

Comtesse, Marquise, Frontin, Chevalier.

MARQUISE: Forgive me for interrupting you, Comtesse. It's occurred to me that you might be delaying your marriage with the Chevalier out of consideration for me. I'm grateful for your concern, but I don't need it. Proceed, Comtesse, today rather than tomorrow. It is I who beg you. Goodbye.

COMTESSE: One moment, Marquise. Tell me if it's true that you and Dorante love each other, that I may rejoice.

MARQUISE: Rejoice without fear. The news is good.

COMTESSE: *(Laughing)* Is it?

MARQUISE: It is, Comtesse, so do hurry. Goodbye.

             She leaves.

SCENE NINE

Chevalier, Comtesse, Frontin.

COMTESSE: *(Laughing)* Ha! Ha! Watch her run, she can't bear to be laughed at. What a pitiful role vanity makes some women play. This one's dying of vexation.

CHEVALIER: She is indeed quivering with it.

FRONTIN: That face Dorante was making, I've just seen it reflected on hers. *(To the Chevalier.)* Please speak about Lisette for me.

COMTESSE: What about Lisette?

FRONTIN: It's a small request I have. Could you take Lisette away from Arlequin and transfer her to me?

CHEVALIER: That's it.

COMTESSE: Is Lisette willing?

FRONTIN: The transfer is completely to her taste.

COMTESSE: I've just had an idea: The Marquise deserves to be punished for all her little plots. Let's see if Dorante, who loves her so much, will mind what I'm about to do. He and I had always agreed Lisette was to marry his valet, Arlequin. I'll tell her to marry Frontin and if Dorante doesn't object, it means he's forgetting me. *(To Frontin.)* Go and find Lisette and her father.

FRONTIN: That's not difficult. They're here.

SCENE TEN

Blaise, Lisette, Chevalier, Comtesse, Frontin.

COMTESSE: Master Blaise, your daughter was engaged to Arlequin, but if you're willing to dispose of her according to my wishes, you'll give her to Frontin. Do you hear, Master Blaise?

BLAISE: I hear very well, but there's another scandal going

about here and we're very upset. We've come to beg
for your mercy, that's why we've come.

COMTESSE: What is it? Why is Lisette crying?

LISETTE: My father will tell you.

BLAISE: This is what it is, if you don't mind my telling you.
Arlequin is a lout, but the most loutish of all the louts
involved in these events is Monsieur Dorante and the
Marquise. They've had the slyness to manoeuvre
Arlequin in such a way that now he doesn't want any
more of Lisette. Even though she wants him. As he
would want her, if only he was allowed to want what he
wanted and he didn't have obstacles thrown everywhere
in his course.

COMTESSE: What obstacles?

BLAISE: By the means of a girl they call Marton who's been
invented on the sly by the Marquise to do mischief, so
she could be promised to Arlequin.

COMTESSE: How strange.

BLAISE: Saying, in that way, that they must be married in Paris,
this painted doll and Arlequin, so that this could bring
damage to our child, who will go into a deep decline
from all this malice, which is nothing but a connivance
to ruin our good reputation and yours, to regale
themselves with laughter at the three of us, and it's
about this that I've come to you: to claim Justice.

COMTESSE: I must try to give it to you. Chevalier, this changes
everything: Frontin must forget Lisette. Don't cry,
Lisette, let the Marquise bring forward all the Martons
she chooses, I'll answer for you happiness. Yes, that
woman, of whom I've been so considerate, is trying to
attack me. Dorante has been too polite to object, but I
may still have more power over him than she imagines.

LISETTE: Arlequin has just treated me with an indifference that
was insufferable. It's as if he'd never seen me before.
That's what the Marquise is doing!

BLAISE: To keep my girl from being a Person's wife.

COMTESSE: We'll take care of it.

FRONTIN: But not to my benefit.

CHEVALIER: Comtesse, I listen to you, I hear you, but my mind does not grasp what you are saying. Lisette, lead us out of this strange maze. Aren't you in love with Frontin?

LISETTE: No. I thought I was while Arlequin loved me. But I've realised my mistake since he's left me.

CHEVALIER: What does one answer to so female a heart?

COMTESSE: I find that this female heart is in the right and doesn't deserve your satire. A man loved her, and now tells her he doesn't love her. She's offended, hurt, I see our heart in hers. Yours would feel the same in a similar situation, so would mine. Go, and let me handle this.

BLAISE: I am going to do battle with Monsieur Dorante and the Marquise.

COMTESSE: Trust me. Here's Dorante, I'll talk to him.

SCENE ELEVEN

Dorante, Comtesse, Chevalier.

COMTESSE: Dorante, let's talk a little about the Marquise.

DORANTE: With pleasure, Comtesse.

COMTESSE: Can you tell me, with pleasure, what she thinks she's been doing today?

DORANTE: I can't believe there's anything to criticise in her behaviour.

COMTESSE: I'll help you change your mind.

DORANTE: You know how discreet she is and. . . .

COMTESSE: This woman you praise so doggedly, Dorante, is jealous of me because the Chevalier left her – as if I had anything to do with it! And she's trying to annoy me in petty ways unworthy of the *non-pareil* you think her. She's even stooped to mixing herself up in the affairs of our servants. She knows that we want Arlequin and Lisette to marry and that I've taken an interest in this

marriage. And in her rage, she can think of nothing
better than to throw some Marton in the way. And
what I find most astounding is your part in these
contemptible dealings. You!

DORANTE: Do you think it ever occurred to the Marquise you'd
take offence? Or that I believed you were still
interested in this affair? Arlequin complained that
Lisette was unfaithful to him and that he'd lost his
happiness. One can feel sorry for these people. The
Marquise, out of kindness, offered her maid Marton as
consolation. He accepted, thanked her, that's all there is
to it.

CHEVALIER: I'm convinced no ill was intended. Let the great
nations make peace and the little countries do the
fighting.

COMTESSE: Chevalier, you may express an opinion when you're
asked. Dorante, please let me hear no more of this little
intrigue. I don't like it. I assume that's saying enough.

DORANTE: Let's call someone. Perhaps Arlequin. . . .

COMTESSE: What are you going to do?

DORANTE: We'll send for the Marquise.

COMTESSE: Why do you need to consult her? Whether she
approves or not, you're the one I'm speaking to, you're
the one I'm telling I want this stopped. I don't care
what she thinks.

DORANTE: Please remember that I have to care. I can decide
nothing without her. Would anything be more rude
than to make my valet reject a favour he's already
accepted? I could never behave that way towards her.

COMTESSE: You're hesitating between us? Do you know what
you're doing?

DORANTE: It's because I do know that I hesitate.

CHEVALIER: That's enough of this trio of valets and chambermaids.

COMTESSE: *(Furious)* Then I must ask you to forget the tone I've
just taken with you. It was unsuitable.

DORANTE:	It will always do me honour. I would obey with alacrity, if I could.
COMTESSE:	*(Laughing)* We have nothing more to say to each other. Give me your hand, Chevalier.
CHEVALIER:	*(Giving his hand.)* Take it and never give it back, Comtesse.
DORANTE:	Would you be kind enough to inform me on another matter.
COMTESSE:	*(Turning around.)* I know nothing.
DORANTE:	You know this: are you soon to be the Chevalier's? When can we have the pleasure of seeing you united?
COMTESSE:	You might have that pleasure tonight.
CHEVALIER:	Gently, dear Comtesse, I'm in a fit of delirium, I'm breathless with rapture.
DORANTE:	I'm delighted, Chevalier, I congratulate you.
COMTESSE:	*(Aside)* How infamous.
DORANTE:	*(Aside)* She's blushing.
COMTESSE:	Is that all?
DORANTE:	Yes.
COMTESSE:	*(To the Chevalier.)* Let's go.

SCENE TWELVE

Comtesse, Marquise, Chevalier, Dorante, Arlequin.

MARQUISE:	Comtesse, Master Blaise has spoken to me, and I've come to repair a fault I committed in all innocence. Arlequin, when I offered you Marton, I had no idea it would displease the Comtesse. You must forget her.
ARLEQUIN:	That's all right. I hear Blaise asked for justice and I'm willing to make amends sooner rather than later. Call the notary and if he's not about, I'll accept his clerk.
COMTESSE:	*(To Dorante.)* Send him away. Marquise, I suggest you

keep your word. I'll even pay for the wedding. Let's hear no more about it.

DORANTE: *(To Arlequin.)* Go.

ARLEQUIN: *(Leaving)* There's no escape from Marton! Chevalier, it's all your fault, this damage. You've turned our loves topsyturvy. If you weren't here, my master and I would have quietly married our Comtesse and Lisette. We wouldn't have the Marquise and Marton on our hands. Hi! Hi! Hi!

MARQUISE/
CHEVALIER: *(Laughing)* He! He! He!

COMTESSE: *(Also laughing.)* If his outrageous remarks amuse you so, tell him to continue. What a charming scene!

CHEVALIER: He's gone mad with love.

DORANTE: Go, blockhead.

MARQUISE: So, Comtesse, are we friends again?

COMTESSE: The best friends in the world. You're too kind.

DORANTE: Marquise, the Chevalier and the Comtesse may be married tonight.

MARQUISE: Indeed?

CHEVALIER: Tonight is still a long way away.

DORANTE: Impatience is understandable. But there are so many things to say at the start of such a sweet journey that we'll leave you and look to our own concerns.

MARQUISE: Comtesse, let me kiss you. Chevalier, I congratulate you. Let's go.

SCENE THIRTEEN

Chevalier, Comtesse.

COMTESSE: You're missed, I see. You were held in high regard.

CHEVALIER: I can manage without it, especially tonight.

COMTESSE: Ah! This is too much!

CHEVALIER: You're not changing your mind!

COMTESSE: A little.

CHEVALIER: What are you considering?

COMTESSE: I have a plan . . . you must help me . . . I'll tell you later. Don't follow me. *(She goes and comes back.)* It's even necessary for us not to see each other for a while. I'll let you know when I need you.

CHEVALIER: I'm stupefied. I feel dizzy. This woman is more womanly than any other.

END OF ACT TWO

ACT THREE

SCENE ONE

Chevalier, Lisette, Frontin.

CHEVALIER: Please ask if I may see her for a moment.

LISETTE: I can't, she's resting.

CHEVALIER: Does she rest standing up?

FRONTIN: I just saw her walking in the gallery.

LISETTE: So? Each has a different way of resting. What method do you use?

CHEVALIER: It seems you're making fun of me, Lisette.

FRONTIN: It seems that way to me.

LISETTE: No, the question was pertinent, and I asked it to keep the conversation going.

CHEVALIER: I have a slight suspicion that you do not like me.

FRONTIN: I had that suspicion as well, but I've exchanged it for an enormous certainty.

LISETTE: Your shrewdness has lost nothing in the exchange.

CHEVALIER: How is it I feel so friendly towards you, and your heart refuses to reciprocate? Why are our feelings so divergent?

LISETTE: Perhaps life requires variety.

FRONTIN: I believe we're also at variance.

LISETTE: If you still love me, yes. If not, we're much of a sameness.

CHEVALIER: Tell me the truth, you don't recommend me to your mistress.

LISETTE: I do: to her indifference.

FRONTIN: What a touching service.

CHEVALIER:	So you're causing her to be gravely prejudiced against me?
LISETTE:	As much as I can. But only by speaking against you. I want her not to love you, I confess it, I never deceive anyone.
FRONTIN:	That's certainly speaking with sincerity.
CHEVALIER:	Ah, Lisette, let's be friends.
LISETTE:	No, do as I do: don't like me.
CHEVALIER:	I want you to like me, and by God, you will like me, I undertake it, I swear it.
LISETTE:	You won't keep your word.
FRONTIN:	Some hatreds won't leave until they've been paid.
CHEVALIER:	How much will the departure of yours cost me?
LISETTE:	Nothing. It's not for sale.
CHEVALIER:	*(Offering his purse.)* Take it, and keep it.
LISETTE:	No, I'd be stealing your money.
CHEVALIER:	Take it, and tell me only what your mistress has in mind.
LISETTE:	No, but I'll tell you what I'd like her to have in mind. Are you intrigued?
FRONTIN:	You've already told us in ten different ways, my beauty.
CHEVALIER:	Does she have a plan?
LISETTE:	Who doesn't? No one goes about without a plan. For example, my plan is to leave you, if your plan is not to leave me.
CHEVALIER:	Let us retreat, Frontin, I feel my anger rising.
FRONTIN:	Goodbye unfriendly chambermaid. Goodbye whimsical little heart, goodbye enchanting weathervane.

They leave.

SCENE TWO

Lisette, Arlequin.

ARLEQUIN: My love, I keep signalling to my master but he ignores me.

LISETTE: You'll have to speak to him in front of the Marquise.

ARLEQUIN: That ill-omened Marquise. Alas, dear girl, my good deed in giving you back my heart will benefit neither one of us. The devil has undertaken to make me marry Marton, he won't budge.

LISETTE: Tell your master I'm waiting for him.

ARLEQUIN: He won't care about your waiting.

LISETTE: We mustn't lose time. Go.

ARLEQUIN: I'm benumbed with sadness.

LISETTE: Shake yourself out of it, since you love me. There's your master with the Marquise. Take him to the side.

            She leaves.

SCENE THREE

Dorante, Arlequin, Marquise.

DORANTE: What is it?

ARLEQUIN: *(To Dorante.)* Let me talk to you, come.

DORANTE: Tell me what you want.

ARLEQUIN: The Marquise mustn't hear.

DORANTE: I have no secrets from her.

ARLEQUIN: But I have one that doesn't want to be known by her.

MARQUISE: Is it such a great mystery?

ARLEQUIN: Yes: Lisette wants to speak to my master and you're not supposed to know it.

MARQUISE: Your discretion is praiseworthy. See what it is,

Dorante, but let me have a word with you first. And you, go and find Lisette.

SCENE FOUR

Dorante, Marquise.

MARQUISE: It seems to be on behalf of the Comtesse.

DORANTE: You see how disturbed she is.

MARQUISE: And you can't wait to surrender.

DORANTE: Does it become me to be cruel?

MARQUISE: We've almost reached our ends. We'll fail if you go so fast. Don't be deceived, the Comtesse's agitation is still ambiguous. I fear there may be more jealousy of me than of your love. The plan may be to win, and make fools of us both. We've taken our measures, let's follow through to the marriage contract, as agreed. Only that moment will show whether or not you're loved. Love behaves one way, pride another. Love sighs for what it has lost. Pride despises what it has been refused: let's wait for the sighs, or the contempt. Hold on until that test, for the sake of your love. Be brief with Lisette, and come back.

DORANTE: Your test makes me tremble, but it's sensible, and I'll see it through.

MARQUISE: My own role is not pleasant and it'll be even less so as we go on! I'll have to compensate for your lack of courage. But what won't one do for revenge? Goodbye.

She leaves.

SCENE FIVE

Dorante, Arlequin, Lisette.

DORANTE: What do you want, Lisette? I only have a moment. You see that I've just left the Marquise, and in my circumstances, our conversation could be misconstrued.

LISETTE: Ah, what could these circumstances be?

DORANTE: I'm going to marry her, that's all.

ARLEQUIN: You're not.

LISETTE: You, marry her!

ARLEQUIN: Never.

DORANTE: Quiet. Don't keep me, Lisette. What do you want?

LISETTE: Gently. Give yourself time to breathe. You're so changed!

ARLEQUIN: It's that traitress who's upset him, but it'll pass.

LISETTE: Don't you remember that I belong to the Comtesse? Have you forgotten her as well?

DORANTE: I have a high regard for her. I respect her. Now, if you don't finish, I'll leave.

LISETTE: Well, I'll finish then. Men!

DORANTE: (Leaving) Goodbye.

ARLEQUIN: Run after him.

LISETTE: Wait. Please.

DORANTE: That exclamation of yours was so out of place. I blush for your mistress.

ARLEQUIN: That's right. It was brazen to say that in front of us. Cancel it.

LISETTE: It's on behalf of my mistress I've come. She wishes to talk to you.

DORANTE: What! Now?

LISETTE: Yes.

ARLEQUIN: The sooner the better.

DORANTE: Will you keep quiet! Have you made your peace with Lisette?

ARLEQUIN: I myself didn't want to. Love wanted it, and Love is the master.

DORANTE: That's your business. Lisette, tell the Comtesse I must ask her to put off our meeting. Beg her forgiveness, but she will approve me herself when I explain my reasons.

LISETTE: She must speak to you. She wants to speak to you.

ARLEQUIN: And here I am, begging you on both knees. Go, this good lady is reformed. I'm sure she'll have excellent things to say to renew your love.

DORANTE: I think you've lost your mind. Lisette, you see that I can't go to the Comtesse. It would disturb the Marquise. The Comtesse is too sensible not to understand that. Anyway, she won't have anything urgent to say.

LISETTE: Nothing, except that she still loves you.

ARLEQUIN: And very much, despite that little parenthesis which took place in the past.

DORANTE: That she still loves me! Lisette, that's too much, if you're speaking for her. And her desire to see me would be too malicious. That the Comtesse abandoned me, that she stopped loving me, as you once told me yourself, I can accept. I wasn't worthy of her. But that she should, out of the giddiness of her heart, try to force me into a quarrel with the Marquise, that's too much! I'll only see her with the person I'm about to join.

He leaves.

ARLEQUIN: (*Following him.*) No, no, dear master, don't take it amiss. And don't miss the right path. Come this way. I'll shout until he hears me.

SCENE SIX

Lisette (alone for a moment), Comtesse.

LISETTE: It must be said my mistress deserves this.

COMTESSE: Is he coming?

LISETTE: No.

COMTESSE: No!

LISETTE: He asks to be excused and says this meeting would
            upset the Marquise, and he's to marry her.

COMTESSE: What are you saying? Marry the Marquise? Him?

LISETTE: Yes, and he's convinced you'll agree that's a valid
            reason for not meeting you.

COMTESSE: This is unbelievable. Are you speaking of Dorante?

LISETTE: Yes, but of a Dorante who no longer loves you.

COMTESSE: That's not true. I couldn't get used to that idea. My
            heart and my reason tell me it's false.

LISETTE: Your heart and your reason are wrong. Dorante even
            suspects you only want to see him to set him at odds
            with the Marquise.

COMTESSE: Leave this everlasting Marquise out of this. She's not
            the woman to make Dorante forget me.

LISETTE: She's only too lovely.

COMTESSE: Too lovely? Are you mad?

LISETTE: At least she can please. Add your unfaithfulness, and
            it's enough to cure Dorante.

COMTESSE: What unfaithfulness?

LISETTE: You yourself told me about it. First you denied it was
            an unfaithfulness because you didn't love Dorante, so
            you said. Then you proved it was harmless. Finally,
            you praised it, and praised it so well I started to imitate
            you. I've since repented.

COMTESSE: I was wrong. I was speaking of unfaithfulness without
            knowing what it was.

LISETTE: Why did you spare no cruelty to drive Dorante away?

COMTESSE: I don't know, but I love him and you're hurting me. I
            treated him badly, I confess, I'm wrong, terribly wrong.
            It's a wrong I'll never forgive myself for, and it doesn't
            deserve to be forgotten. What more do you want me to say?
            I behaved badly, that's true.

LISETTE: That's what I told you before you won me over.

COMTESSE:	Miserable female pride, o unfortunate need to be loved; that's what you're costing me. I wanted the Chevalier to love me, as if it were worth the trouble. I needed that tribute to my charms. They can boast now! I've won the Chevalier and I've lost Dorante.
LISETTE:	What a difference!
COMTESSE:	Worse: if I listened to my nature, I would detest the Chevalier. I've always found him absurd, and now he's the one left in the place of the most desirable man in the world. Ah, I'm in a fine state!
LISETTE:	Don't waste any more time distressing yourself. Dorante doesn't know you still love him. Are you going to leave him to the Marquise? Why not try to get him back? Since he has the right to be angry, and you're in the wrong, make a few gestures towards him.
COMTESSE:	What can I do with a wretch who won't even talk to me? I'll have to give him up. Is that a way to behave? You say he has a right to be angry, but Lisette, did I imagine he'd abandon me? Did I suspect him of such cowardice? Has anyone ever relied on a heart as much as I did on his? Infinite respect, blind trust, and you say I'm in the wrong? Isn't a man false-hearted when he betrays such feelings. I had them, Lisette.
LISETTE:	I don't understand anything.
COMTESSE:	I wasn't worried by his lamentations and jealousies. I laughed at his recriminations, I challenged his heart to fail me. My idea was not to spare him. No woman has ever lived in such a state of security. I congratulated myself, because this showed him to such advantage. And after that, this man leaves me! Isn't he unforgivable?
LISETTE:	Calm down. You're so unhappy, I can't bear it. Let's work at getting him back and not rail in vain against him. Begin by breaking off with the Chevalier. I've already sent him away twice.
COMTESSE:	I told that importunate man not to come until I called him.
LISETTE:	What will you do with him?

COMTESSE: Hate him to the full extent of his hatefulness. That's
             what I have in store for him. Still, I need him in all
             this. Let him come. You can even fetch him.

LISETTE: Let's see what my father wants first.

SCENE SEVEN

Blaise, Comtesse, Lisette.

BLAISE: Are you aware of what's happening here? Have you
             been warned about a legal personality who's walking in
             the garden with Monsieur Dorante and the Marquise,
             and who says he's brought some rag of a contract
             which they ordered from him, in order that they can
             end up thrusting themselves together in front of his
             legal person? What do you say to that, Comtesse?
             Because my daughter says your affection for Monsieur
             Dorante has sprouted again. And this legal personality
             is an impertinent.

COMTESSE: A notary in my house. Lisette, do they want to marry
             here?

BLAISE: There's no doubt about that. They also say he can
             make a contract for four people. That is, one for
             Dorante, your lover who is past, with the Marquise,
             and one with you and the Chevalier, your admirer of
             the present. That's how they're making merry of all
             this and it makes me very angry. And you?

COMTESSE: I don't understand. It's like a dream.

LISETTE: A disgusting nightmare.

BLAISE: This Marquise, despite her noble title, is not acting in a
             straight and narrow way. One doesn't go about thieving
             the lovers of a person of your kind. There's only one
             useful word here: I have my rake at the ready and as
             soon as you speak, I'll rake up that notary and his
             pieces of paper no more no less than I would a weed.

COMTESSE: Say something, Lisette, help me! They'll marry each
             other here if I don't do something. It's no longer about

Dorante, you see that I hate him, but I'm being insulted.

LISETTE: I'm as angry as you are and in your place I'd no longer bother with him.

COMTESSE: But if you loved him!

LISETTE: You say you hate him!

COMTESSE: That doesn't keep me from loving him. And then, why hate him? He thinks I'm in the wrong, you said so yourself, and you were right. I abandoned him first. I must find him and undeceive him.

BLAISE: There was a time when he cherished me. Do you consider it'll be a good thing if I talk to him?

COMTESSE: I should write him a note. Your father could give it to him without the Marquise knowing.

LISETTE: Do that.

COMTESSE: Actually, I wrote one earlier, I have it here. Blaise, try to keep the Marquise from noticing it.

BLAISE: There will be no noticing. And while he's in the reading of your letter, I'll reinforce it with some exhortations.

He leaves.

SCENE EIGHT

Frontin, Chevalier, Lisette, Comtesse.

CHEVALIER: Comtesse, what's become of love? What does the heart think? Is this how you tell me to come? What's your motive for our separation? You didn't send for me, you let me languish, I sent for myself.

COMTESSE: I was about to send for you.

CHEVALIER: The messenger seemed late. What have you decided? Our friends are about to marry, the contract is being drawn up at this moment. Why not use the notary? They've delegated me to suggest this. Remember that love groans when it must wait, that the needs of the heart are urgent, that the moments are precious, that the ones you are stealing from me are irreplaceable, and that I'm dying. Forward then.

COMTESSE: No, Chevalier, that is not my plan.

CHEVALIER: We will not marry?

COMTESSE: No.

CHEVALIER: What does that mean, no?

COMTESSE: No signifies no. I want to reconcile you with the Marquise.

CHEVALIER: But it's you I love.

COMTESSE: But I do not love you at all. I'm sorry to tell you this so abruptly, but you ought to know it.

CHEVALIER: You're teasing me!

COMTESSE: I'm speaking in all seriousness.

CHEVALIER: Comtesse, enough. Don't play with a heart that will perish from terror.

COMTESSE: You must have known my feelings. I've always put off this marriage. Why didn't you guess I didn't want to go through with it?

CHEVALIER: The summit of my happiness was fixed for tonight.

COMTESSE: You may still have the summit of your happiness tonight, with the Marquise.

CHEVALIER: What do the Marquise and the Chevalier have to do with each other?

COMTESSE: They have to love each other, as they once did. I can offer you no other course of action, I'll take it upon myself to reconcile you.

CHEVALIER: This is a passing fancy.

COMTESSE: It's an everlasting feeling.

LISETTE: I guarantee its eternity.

CHEVALIER: Frontin, where are we?

FRONTIN: A general survey indicates we're nowhere. This path does not lead to a welcoming roof.

LISETTE: It does: follow this path and you'll end up back home.

CHEVALIER: Am I to leave, Comtesse? Is that the end?

COMTESSE: I'm waiting for an answer to a letter. You'll know all
              when I've received it. Delay your departure until then.

SCENE NINE

Arlequin, Frontin, Chevalier, Lisette, Comtesse.

ARLEQUIN: My master and the Marquise have sent me to ask if
              they might disturb you. They've come to destroy your
              hopes and mine. I can't marry Lisette now that my
              master doesn't want you.

COMTESSE: I'm expecting them . . . *(To Lisette.)* He hasn't received
              my letter. What I'll tell them will put you in the
              picture, Chevalier, and it won't be my fault if you're
              not happy.

CHEVALIER: I've been taken in, that's the picture.

SCENE TEN

*Marquise, Dorante, Comtesse, Chevalier, Frontin, Arlequin, Lisette,
Blaise.*

MARQUISE: I see nothing that announces a marriage with the
              Chevalier, Comtesse. When do you propose to complete
              his happiness?

COMTESSE: When you wish, Marquise, his happiness is in your
              hands.

MARQUISE: Mine, Comtesse? Then marry him today and allow us
              to add our marriage to yours.

COMTESSE: Are you getting married? Has someone come here to
              marry you, Marquise?

MARQUISE: *(Showing Dorante.)* He's already here.

DORANTE: The Marquise has done me the honour of giving me her hand. As we're in your house, we've come to ask your permission to marry here.

COMTESSE: The request does me too much honour. But I believe Heaven has another fate in store for you.

CHEVALIER: We've changed the distribution of things, Dorante. I've fallen to the lot of the Marquise, the Comtesse falls to you.

MARQUISE: We'll remain as we are.

COMTESSE: Let me speak, Marquise. I demand a hearing. It's time to be undeceived. Chevalier, you thought I loved you: the warmth with which I received you might have misled you, but it was never so. I always loved Dorante, and I bore with you only to test his heart. This has cost you some pain, you love me, and I'm sorry. But your love served my plan. Marquise, you have a right to complain, the Chevalier allowed himself to be distracted from the love he owed you. But his fault is excusable and I can't be vain for having taken him away from you for a time. He didn't succumb to my charms, but to my skills: he didn't find me lovelier than you, only more predisposed towards him, and that's always an allurement. Dorante, you stood a test conceived with such tenderness rather badly. I have little cause to be satisfied, but perhaps your present behaviour owes more to resentment than to a lukewarm love. I went a little far, you might have misunderstood me. I won't judge you harshly, I'll close my eyes and forgive you.

MARQUISE: *(Laughing)* Ha! Ha! Ha! It's too late, Comtesse, at least I flatter myself it is. You can be even more generous and forgive the knots that are about to unite us.

COMTESSE: Dorante, you'll lose me forever if you hesitate for a moment.

CHEVALIER: I demand a hearing: I'm losing the Marquise and have no right to complain. I was lacking in faithfulness. I don't know how, because her qualities gave it more than enough encouragement. It's beyond me how I came to this unhappy pass. In a word, I'm unfaithful, I confess to it. But I'm truthful, I boast of it. I could

retaliate, and say to the Comtesse: You deceived me, I
deceived you. But I'm only a man, I don't aspire to
such subtlety. Here is the exact account: you imitated
love, Comtesse, so you say. I wasn't worthy of more.
But there was more. Don't retract the fatal honour you
did me: I loved you, you more than returned it.

COMTESSE: That's what you believed.

CHEVALIER: I conclude: I loved you a little less than the Marquise.
I'll explain: she had more of my heart, I adored her.
But I loved you, by God, with some memories of her.
Yes, Dorante, we were moving in the sphere of love.
Don't believe anything else, my friend. The Comtesse
is vexed because you're leaving her and her allurements
have proven inferior. Her pride cries out, reclaims you,
plays the siren: be deaf to her song. *(Showing the
Marquise.)* Let those beautiful eyes be your antidote.
Stay with her, who's been well revenged by my pain. I
don't say this easily, I'd fight for her with my last drop
of blood, had I that right. Take her, Dorante, and
thank heaven for your happiness. Of all brides, the
most worthy of respect and love is yours; of all losses,
the greatest is mine; and of all men, the most
treacherous, disloyal, and at the same time most stupid,
is the unhappy one speaking to you now.

MARQUISE: I can add nothing to that definition. It's all there.

COMTESSE: I won't condescend to answer your accusations,
Chevalier, they were spoken in spite. I told you my
intentions, Dorante. If you're not worthy of them, we
won't mention it again.

MARQUISE: We love each other in good faith, Comtesse, there's no
going back. Two people who have been forgotten have
the right to marry elsewhere. You two must try to
forget us once again, it'll be easier this time, you've had
practice. Here's the contract, Dorante. Please ask the
Comtesse to have the kindness to sign it.

COMTESSE: So soon?

MARQUISE: Yes, Comtesse, with your permission.

COMTESSE: I'm speaking to Dorante.

DORANTE: Yes, Comtesse.

COMTESSE: I wouldn't have believed it.

MARQUISE: We're even hoping to see yours next to it. And you, Chevalier, won't you sign?

CHEVALIER: I've forgotten how to write.

MARQUISE: Here's a pen for the Comtesse.

COMTESSE: *(Quickly)* Give it to me. *(She signs and throws the pen away.)* Ah! Traitor!

DORANTE: *(Throwing himself on his knees.)* Ah! Comtesse!

MARQUISE: Surrender, Dorante, you're loved.

ARLEQUIN: What a pleasure, Lisette.

LISETTE: I'm delighted.

COMTESSE: What! Dorante at my feet?

DORANTE: More loving than ever.

COMTESSE: Get up. Dorante still loves me?

DORANTE: And never stopped loving you.

COMTESSE: And the Marquise?

DORANTE: I'll owe your heart to her, if you give it back. She managed everything.

COMTESSE: I can breathe. What pain you caused me. How can you have pretended for so long?

DORANTE: Love gave me the strength. I hoped to win back what I adore.

COMTESSE: *(Forcefully)* Where is the Marquise that I may kiss her.

MARQUISE: *(Coming close and kissing her.)* Here, Comtesse. Are we good friends?

COMTESSE: I owe you my happiness and good sense.

Dorante kisses the Comtesse's hand.

MARQUISE: As for you, Chevalier, I advise you to give your hand elsewhere. It seems no one here wants it.

COMTESSE: No, Marquise, I'll obtain his grace. My joy would be incomplete without it.

MARQUISE: We'll see in six months.

CHEVALIER: I only ask for a reprieve. The rest is up to me.

They leave.

SCENE ELEVEN

Frontin, Lisette, Blaise, Arlequin.

FRONTIN: Are you marrying Arlequin, Lisette?

LISETTE: My heart tells me so.

ARLEQUIN: Mine is of the same opinion.

BLAISE: My will goes on top of that.

FRONTIN: I give you six months to come back to me.

THE END

LA DISPUTE

LA DISPUTE was performed on BBC Radio 3 in 1987. The cast was as follows:

HERMIANE	Maggie McCarthy
THE PRINCE	Ronald Herdman
MESROU	Alton Kumalo
CARISE	Valerie Murray
EGLE	Maureen O'Brien
AZOR	Gary Cady
ADINE	Jane Leonard
MESRIN	James Macpherson
DIRECTOR	David Johnston
MUSIC	Gordon Langford

CHARACTERS

HERMIANE

THE PRINCE

MESROU

CARISE

EGLE

AZOR

ADINE

MESRIN

MESLIS

DINA

COURTIERS

The action takes place in the country.

SCENE ONE

The Prince, Hermiane, Carise, Mesrou.

HERMIANE: Where are you taking me, your Highness? This country looks wild and isolated and I see no signs of the entertainment you promised me.

THE PRINCE: *(Laughing)* Everything will be ready.

HERMIANE: I don't understand. What is that strange building over there? What is the meaning of those extraordinarily high walls around it? Where are we going?

THE PRINCE: We are going to watch an unusual spectacle, Hermiane. Remember the question we discussed last night: you maintained against the whole of my court that it was not your sex but ours which had first been unfaithful in love.

HERMIANE: Yes, your Highness, and I still maintain it. The first unfaithfulness could only have been committed by someone who was bold enough to blush at nothing. Now, ever since the beginning of this corrupt world, women have been – and still are – naturally timid and reserved. How then could they be the first to fall into a pattern of vicious behaviour that requires such daring, such libertine feelings and such insolence? No, your Highness, it doesn't make sense.

THE PRINCE: Indeed, Hermiane, it doesn't make sense to me either and you needn't argue with me on that subject. I share your feelings against everyone else, as you know.

HERMIANE: Yes, but I'm afraid that is only out of gallantry, your Highness.

THE PRINCE: Gallantry? I haven't noticed it, Hermiane. It is true that I love you and perhaps that fact helped to convince me you were right, but this has happened in such a subtle way I've not been aware of it. I have no respect for the hearts of men: deal with them as you will. I'm certain man's heart is indeed more unfaithful than a woman's. Mine alone must be excepted from this rule and that is only because it is you who are the object of my love. If it were anyone else it would no longer be so.

HERMIANE: Your words betray irony, your Highness.

THE PRINCE: Then I shall be punished soon enough. You will soon have the means to silence me if you find I don't agree with you.

HERMIANE: What do you mean?

THE PRINCE: We must look to Nature for our answers. Surely only Nature can decide once and for all who was the first to be unfaithful and I'm certain her decision will prove us right.

HERMIANE: Please explain yourself.

THE PRINCE: There is only one way to know whether the two of us are right in believing that it was a man who was responsible for the first unfaithfulness: and that is to be there at the beginning of the world.

HERMIANE: Quite. But we weren't.

THE PRINCE: No, but we will be. We will soon watch men and women exactly as they were at the beginning. Ah, here we are. Carise, Mesrou, is everything ready?

CARISE/
MESROU: Yes, your Highness.

THE PRINCE: Hermiane, the world and its first loves are about to appear before us exactly as they were, or at least as they must have been. The events may not be precisely the same, but the characters will be. You are about to see hearts in the same state they were at the beginning of the world and souls as fresh as in those first days, or even more fresh. Carise, Mesrou, you may go now. Warn us when you are about to begin.

CARISE/
MESROU: Yes, your Highness.

THE PRINCE: Come this way, Hermiane.

SCENE TWO

Hermiane, The Prince.

HERMIANE: You've excited my curiosity, your Highness.

THE PRINCE: I'll explain. Some eighteen or nineteen years ago the dispute we had yesterday took place at my father's court. It lasted a long time and became heated. My father disagreed with our view, Hermiane, but he was a man of science and decided to make a foolproof experiment. He found four new born babies and had them taken to this forest. Two of them were of your sex and two of mine. He gave each one of them extensive grounds and built separate houses for them in which they still live. In that way, none ever met any of the others and they know only Mesrou and his sister Carise who brought them up and still care for them. My father chose black people as their guardians so that they'd be even more surprised when they met each other. Today, for the first time, these young people will be given the freedom to leave their enclosures and meet one another. They speak our language and we can listen to their conversation, which will be the same as it was in the beginning of the world. The first loves are about to begin, Hermiane. Let us watch what happens.

(Sound of trumpets.)

There's the fanfare. Our young people are about to appear. This gallery runs along the whole building; we'll watch them unseen and listen.

SCENE THREE

Carise, Eglé.

CARISE: Don't be afraid, Eglé. Follow me.

EGLE: Oh, Carise, where are we going?

CARISE: Look: here are grounds you've never seen before. You can walk through them without danger.

EGLE: What do I see, Carise? So many new worlds!

CARISE: No it's always the same world. You didn't know how big it was.

EGLE: Look at all these countries, these dwellings. I feel very small in such a wide space. I like it, but it frightens me as well. *(She looks and stops by a stream.)* Oh, look, Carise. What's this water rolling on the ground. I've never seen such a thing happen in my world.

CARISE: That's called a stream.

EGLE: *(Looking)* Carise, come here, quickly. Look. There's something living in the stream. It looks like a person. It seems to be as surprised by me as I am by it.

CARISE: *(Laughing)* It's yourself you're seeing. All streams do that.

EGLE: That's me? There? That's my face?

CARISE: Yes.

EGLE: But do you know that it's very beautiful. Yes, it is a most enchanting object. If only I'd known that before!

CARISE: It's true that you are beautiful, Eglé.

EGLE: Beautiful? I'm absolutely ravishing. What a delightful discovery. Look, the stream repeats all of my expressions and there's not one I don't like. You and Mesrou must have been very happy to look at me all these years. I could spend my whole life looking at myself. Oh, I'm going to love myself very much from now on.

CARISE: I have to attend to something in your house, Eglé, do
            you mind staying alone?

EGLE: No, no, I won't be bored as long as the stream stays
            with me.

SCENE FOUR

Eglé is alone for a moment, then Azor appears, facing her.

EGLE: I'm so beautiful I'll never tire of looking at myself. *(She sees Azor.) (Frightened)* Oh. What's this? Another person just like me. No, no, don't come any closer. *(To herself.)* The person laughs. The person seems to be admiring me. *(To Azor.)* Wait, please. Don't move. *(To herself.)* And yet, the person looks at me with such a gentle expression. *(To Azor.)* Can you speak?

AZOR: Yes. It was the pleasure of seeing you that had made me speechless.

EGLE: The person hears me and answers me in a very pleasant manner.

AZOR: You enchant me.

EGLE: Good.

AZOR: You delight me.

EGLE: I like you too.

AZOR: Why then do you forbid me to come any closer?

EGLE: I'm no longer forbidding you with as much conviction as before.

AZOR: Then I'll come closer.

EGLE: Yes, I would enjoy that. No, wait. I'm so agitated.

AZOR: I obey you because I'm yours.

EGLE: The person obeys me! Well then, come a little closer. You can't really be mine if you stay so far away. Ah, yes. It's you. *(To herself.)* The person's very well put together. Do you know, you're almost as beautiful as I am.

AZOR: Being so close to you is making me die of happiness. I want to give myself to you. I don't know what I feel, I don't know how to say it.

EGLE: That's how I feel.

AZOR: I'm happy. I'm fainting.

EGLE: I'm sighing.

AZOR: It doesn't matter how close I am to you, I still can't see enough of you.

EGLE: That's what I think too. But I don't know how we can see more of each other. It's impossible for us to be any closer.

AZOR: My heart wants your hands.

EGLE: Here: take my hands. My heart gives them to you. Are you any happier now?

AZOR: Yes, but not more at peace.

EGLE: Nor am I, we're alike in all things.

AZOR: Oh, no, there's such a difference between us. The whole of me can't even compare with your eyes. They're so soft.

EGLE: But yours are lively.

AZOR: You're so pretty, so delicate.

EGLE: Yes, but I assure you it wouldn't suit you to be as pretty as I am. I wouldn't want you to be any different from the way you are. It's another kind of perfection. I don't deny mine, but you must keep yours.

AZOR: I won't change then.

EGLE: Ah, tell me, where were you before I knew you?

AZOR: In a world of my own. But I won't ever go back there since you don't live there and I want to have your hands with me forever. I can no longer manage without them, nor can my mouth deprive itself of kissing them.

EGLE: And my hands can no longer be deprived of the kisses of your mouth. Shh. I hear a noise. These must be the people from my world. Hide behind this tree or they'll be frightened. I'll call you.

AZOR: But I can't see you from behind that tree.

EGLE: All you need do is look into that water. My face is there, you'll see it.

SCENE FIVE

Mesrou, Carise, Eglé.

EGLE: He's only just gone and I'm already suffering. Ah, Carise.

CARISE: You seem troubled Eglé, what's the matter?

MESROU: Her eyes are softer than usual today.

EGLE: Carise, Mesrou, I have very important news: you believe there are only three of us in this world, but you're wrong: there are four of us. I've acquired an object that was holding my hand a few moments ago.

CARISE: Holding your hand? Why didn't you call for help?

EGLE: Help against what, Carise? Against the pleasure it gave me? I was very pleased to have my hand held. It was being held with my consent. This person kissed my hand all the time and I want to call the person back so it can kiss my hand again and give me and itself all that pleasure.

MESROU: I know who it is. I believe I saw him hiding behind the tree. This object is called a man, Eglé, and his name is Azor. We already know him.

EGLE: Azor? That's Azor? What a lovely name. Dear Azor, dear man. He'll come back soon.

CARISE: I'm not surprised he loves you and that you love him. You were made for each other.

EGLE: Quite. We guessed as much ourselves. *(She calls.)* Azor, my Azor, come here quickly, come here, dear Man.

SCENE SIX

Carise, Eglé, Mesrou, Azor.

AZOR: Carise, Mesrou, you're here. These are friends of mine.

EGLE: *(Cheerfully)* They've just told me. They've also declared you were made on purpose for me and I'm made on purpose for you. That's why we love each other so much. I'm your Eglé, and you're my Azor.

MESROU: One is the man, the other the woman.

EGLE: Here's my hand, Azor. It'll make up for your having had to hide. *(To Carise and Mesrou.)* That's what he was doing with my hand before. You see there wasn't any need to call for help, was there?

CARISE: Children, I've told you already that your destiny is to be enchanted by one another.

EGLE: *(Holding Azor's hand.)* That's obvious.

CARISE: But if you want to love each other forever, you'll have to observe one rule.

EGLE: Yes, I know. To be always in each other's company.

CARISE: No: the opposite. You must occasionally deprive yourselves of the happiness of seeing each other.

EGLE: How now?

AZOR: What?

CARISE: Yes. If you don't observe this rule you'll soon see this happiness diminish and you'll become indifferent to one another.

EGLE: *(Laughing)* Indifferent! My Azor indifferent? Hahaha. What an amusing thought. Hahah.

AZOR: *(Laughing)* How little Carise knows.

MESROU: Don't laugh at Carise, she's giving you excellent advice. It's only by doing what she suggests, that is by separating occasionally that Carise and I have continued to love each other

EGLE: Yes, that might work for you. You're both so black you must have run away in terror the first time you saw each other. Hahaha.

AZOR: The best the two of you could hope for was to learn to tolerate each other.

EGLE: And if you saw each other all the time you'd be repelled because you have nothing beautiful to show each other. I know that I love you, but I never miss you when I don't see you. I don't need your presence at all. Now why is that? It's because you don't please me. But Azor and I are enchanted with each other. He's so handsome and I'm so lovely, so appealing, we're transported every time we look at each other.

AZOR: Let me have your hand again, Eglé. You see how much I suffer when I can't hold her hand. And when I'm holding it I want to die if I can't kiss it, and when I've kissed it I still want to die. And that's only her hand.

EGLE: The man is right and I feel everything he's described. in the same way. That's what's happened to us and when you talk about our happiness you do it without understanding anything about it. Even we who feel this happiness don't understand it. It's – infinite.

MESROU: We're only asking you to separate for two or three hours a day.

EGLE: No. We can't manage a minute.

MESROU: What a pity.

EGLE: You're beginning to irritate me, Mesrou. What will happen if Azor and I see too much of each other? Will we become ugly? Will we stop being enchanting?

CARISE: No, but you'll stop feeling that you are.

EGLE: How can we possibly stop feeling something that we are?

AZOR: Eglé will always be my Eglé.

EGLE: And Azor always my Azor.

MESROU: Yes, we understand that, but you don't know what

might happen. Suppose I were to become as handsome
as Azor or that Carise were suddenly as beautiful as
Eglé.

EGLE: Why should we care about that?

CARISE: If you'd had a surfeit of seeing each other, you might
             be tempted to leave one another and to love us.

EGLE: Why should we be tempted? Does one leave what one
             loves? What sort of thinking is that? Azor and I love
             each other, that's all there is to it. You may become as
             beautiful as you wish, what does it matter to us? That
             will be your concern. We already have ours.

AZOR: Carise and Mesrou will never understand. They would
             have to be in our place to know what has happened.

MESROU: As you wish.

AZOR: My love is my life, Mesrou.

EGLE: Have you heard that, Carise. His life. How can he leave
             me? He has to live, and so do I.

AZOR: Yes, my life. Ah, how is it possible to be so beautiful,
             to have such beautiful eyes, such a beautiful mouth, to
             have everything so beautiful?

EGLE: I love it when he admires me.

MESROU: He does adore you.

AZOR: Yes, Mesrou, you've said that very well. I adore.
             Mesrou finally understands me. Eglé, I adore you.

EGLE: (Gasping.) Adore me, Azor, but let me breathe a little.
             Ah, that's better.

CARISE: I'm delighted to see so much tenderness between you,
             but you will not preserve it unless you listen to us. You
             must make an effort to be wise. Eglé, give this portrait
             to Azor. It will make your absence easier for him to
             bear.

EGLE: What's this? Ah, it's me. Yes, I recognise myself. It's a
             much better image of me than the one in the stream.
             All of my beauty is there; yes, it's very much me. How
             wonderful it is to find oneself everywhere. Look Azor,
             look at my attractions.

AZOR:	It's Eglé, it's my beloved woman. But it's not as beautiful as the real Eglé.
MESROU:	At least it represents her.
AZOR:	Yes, it does. Let me kiss the portrait then. *(He kisses it.)* It only makes me want the real Eglé more.
EGLE:	Yes and there's another problem. When he kisses the portrait, it's my copy who has everything. I have nothing.
AZOR:	Give me your hand and I'll make amends.
EGLE:	I want a portrait of Azor to play with.
MESROU:	You can have his portrait or your own. Which one would you prefer?
EGLE:	I'll have both, please.
MESROU:	You have to choose one: I want to keep the other.
EGLE:	I suppose I don't really need Azor's portrait because I already have his image in my mind. I'll take my own portrait then and that way I can have both images together.
CARISE:	Here is another kind of portrait. It's called a mirror and if you push this button here, it will open. We must leave now. We'll come back in a little while. In the meantime, please remember what we said about short separations.

SCENE SEVEN

Azor, Eglé.

EGLE: I can't open the box, Azor, why don't you try? Carise said to push this button.

AZOR: *(Opening it and looking.)* There. But I only see myself in there. Yes, it's the same face I saw in the stream.

EGLE: Let me see. No, Azor, you're wrong. Look. It's me again. It's your Eglé exactly as she is. Come and see for yourself.

AZOR: You're right. It is you. No, wait. Look, now there are two of us in there. Half you and half me. I'd prefer it to be just you, I can't see as much of you when I'm in there as well.

EGLE: I like seeing a little of you in there. You don't spoil anything, I assure you. Come a little closer. Stay still.

AZOR: Our faces look as if they're about to touch in there. Now they are touching. What happiness for my face.

EGLE: I can feel your face and I like it.

AZOR: What if our mouths were to come a little closer?

They kiss.

EGLE: Look, you've disturbed us in there and I can only see myself now. This mirror is an admirable invention.

AZOR: So is the portrait, I want to kiss it again.

He kisses it.

EGLE: Azor, do you think Carise and Mesrou are good people?

AZOR: Yes, I do and they wish us the very best. I wanted to talk to you about the advice they gave us.

EGLE: About those separations? I was thinking about that as well.

AZOR: Yes, my Eglé. Their predictions have frightened me. I'm not worried as far as I'm concerned, but I don't want you to become bored with me. I'd be desperate if that ever happened.

EGLE: Yes, but you must also take care of yourself. You must never tire of adoring me. I know I'm beautiful but now your fears have frightened me.

AZOR: No, no. *You* needn't be afraid. Eglé . . . what are you thinking about now?

EGLE: I've taken everything into consideration and come to a decision. Let's cause ourselves some pain and agree to separate for two hours. Your heart and its adoration of me mean even more to me than your presence.
Although I also like your presence very much.

AZOR: What? Separate? Us?

EGLE: Ah, Azor, we must separate immediately. If we wait even a moment, I'll no longer want to part from you.

AZOR: Alas, I don't have the strength to separate.

EGLE: And I'm rapidly losing mine. *(Azor starts crying.)* Are you crying, my poor Azor? Stay then. As long as there's no danger.

AZOR: But you said there was a danger.

EGLE: Then go.

AZOR: Yes, I'll go. Goodbye, Eglé. Goodbye.

SCENE EIGHT

Eglé, alone.

EGLE: Alas, he's gone. I'm all alone. I can no longer hear his voice. *(She sighs.)* Azor. Azor. I ought never to have sent my man away. *(She looks at herself in the mirror.)* Look at that face. Carise and Mesrou don't know what they are talking about: separations aren't necessary to make someone love that face forever. If only I'd looked at myself more carefully I would have known better than to send Azor away. Azor. . . Oh well, I'll go and sit by the stream again. At least it's another mirror.

SCENE NINE

Eglé, Adine.

ADINE: What's this?

EGLE: Oh. This seems to be yet another person.

ADINE: A new object. I'll get closer and have a look.

EGLE: The person's studying me with care, but it doesn't seem to feel admiration for me. This is not another Azor. *(She looks at herself in the mirror.)* Nor is it an Eglé, no, definitely not. And yet, it seems to be making comparisons.

ADINE: I don't know what to think of that face. It lacks something; it's rather insipid.

EGLE: There's something about this person I don't like.

ADINE: Does it have a language? Let's see. Hm, hm. Are you a person?

EGLE: Yes, I am very much a person.

ADINE: Well? *(Pause)* Have you nothing to say to me?

EGLE: No. People are usually eager to speak to me.

ADINE: But aren't you delighted by me?

EGLE: By you? I am the one who delights others.

ADINE: What? You're not overjoyed to see me?

EGLE: Neither overjoyed nor particularly displeased. Why should I care whether I see you or not?

ADINE: This is very strange. I show myself to you, you look at me. And yet you feel nothing. You must be looking somewhere else by mistake. Gaze upon me with a little more care. Now. How do you find me?

EGLE: You, you, you. Who cares about you? I've already told you that I'm the one who is gazed upon. I'm the one who's spoken to and told about the impression I've made. That's how it is. How can you ask me to look at you when I myself am here?

ADINE: Surely it's the one who is the more beautiful who waits for others to notice her and gaze upon her in astonishment.

EGLE: Then what are you waiting for? Be astonished.

ADINE: Didn't you hear me? I said it was the more beautiful one who waits for the admiration of others.

EGLE: And I've told you the more beautiful one is waiting.

ADINE: If I am not that one, then where is she? There are three people in this world and they are all lost in admiration of me.

EGLE: I know nothing about these people of yours, but there are three who are enchanted with me and who treat me as I deserve to be treated.

ADINE: I know that I am beautiful, so beautiful I delight myself every time I look at myself. You see how things are.

EGLE: What is this tale you're telling me? I who am speaking to you can never look at myself without becoming totally enraptured.

ADINE: Enraptured? I admit you're quite passable, even rather pleasant. You see that I'm not like you and that I'm making an effort to be fair.

EGLE: (Aside) I'd like to beat her with her fairness.

ADINE: You're not seriously thinking of entering into a dispute with me over who is the more beautiful, are you? Why, one need only look.

EGLE: But it's by looking that I find you rather ugly.

ADINE: That's because you can't help finding me beautiful and you're jealous.

EGLE: The only thing that prevents me from finding you beautiful is your face.

ADINE: My face? Oh, you can't vex me that way. I've seen my face. Go and ask the waters of the stream about my face. Ask Mesrin who adores me.

EGLE: The waters of the stream are making fun of you and

they've already told me that there is nothing more
beautiful than my own face. I know nothing about this
Mesrin of yours but he will need only catch a glimpse
of my face to stop looking at you. Furthermore I have
an Azor who's worth much more than your Mesrin, an
Azor I love and who is almost as enchanting as I am.
And he says I am his life. You're nobody's life. *And* I
have a mirror which confirms everything the stream
and Azor have already told me. Can anything beat that?

ADINE: *(Laughing)* A mirror? You have a mirror as well? What
can a mirror do for you except make you look at
yourself. Hahaha.

EGLE: Hahaha. I knew I wouldn't like her.

ADINE: Here. Take a look at this mirror which tells the truth.
Learn to know yourself better and to keep quiet.

EGLE: Why don't you take this one and look at yourself in
there. It will teach you how mediocre you are and to
adopt a tone of modesty when speaking to me.

ADINE: Go away. I have no use for you if you will persist in
your refusal to admire me. I'm turning my back on
you. There.

EGLE: As for me, I don't even know you're here.

ADINE: What a madwoman.

EGLE: She's deluded. What world can such a person have
come from? There's Carise, I'll ask her.

SCENE TEN

Carise, Adine, Eglé.

CARISE: What are you two doing so far apart? Why aren't you talking to each other?

ADINE: That's a new person I've come across. She's been thrown into despair by my beauty.

EGLE: Have you ever seen a duller object than that one over there, Carise? She's a silly person who aspires to astonish me. She keeps asking me what I feel when I look at her. She seems to expect me to be happy when I see her. She actually said to me: "Gaze upon me, how do you find me?" She even has the arrogance to think herself as beautiful as I am.

ADINE: I didn't say that. I said I was more beautiful than you. That's obvious as soon as you look into the mirror.

CARISE: Gently, gently. Don't be angry with each other. You must enjoy being together and add to it the pleasure of knowing yourselves to be both adored. Eglé is adored by Azor whom she cherishes and Adine by Mesrin whom she loves in return. Come, come, be friends.

EGLE: I will as soon as she rids herself of her delusions of beauty.

ADINE: I know how to bring her to her senses. I'll take her Azor away from her, not that I care anything for him, but I'll do anything for a little peace.

EGLE: Where's that idiot friend of hers, Mesrin? If I come across him, she can beware. Goodbye, I must leave. I can't stand her presence any more.

ADINE: Hahaha, It's my merits which cause her aversion.

EGLE: Hahaha. What an unpleasant face.

SCENE ELEVEN

Adine, Carise.

CARISE: Don't pay attention, Adine, let her go.

ADINE: I feel sorry for her, that's all.

CARISE: It's time for your music lesson.

ADINE: I'm coming, but I see Mesrin and I want to have a word with him.

CARISE: But you only left him a moment ago.

ADINE: I'll only be a moment.

SCENE TWELVE

Mesrin, Carise, Adine.

ADINE:	*(Calls)* Mesrin!
MESRIN:	*(Running to her.)* Adine. Ah, it's you. It's my Adine. She's come back to me. I've been so impatient. Oh, I'm so happy.
ADINE:	No, no, restrain your happiness, Mesrin, I haven't come back. I only happened to be here.
MESRIN:	Then you must happen to stay with me, Adine.
CARISE:	Be quick, Adine, or we won't have time for your lesson.
ADINE:	Yes, yes. Mesrin, I am beautiful, am I not?
MESRIN:	Beautiful! Oh, so beautiful!
ADINE:	You see, Carise, he doesn't hesitate. He describes what he sees.
MESRIN:	You are divine, you are beauty incarnate.
ADINE:	Yes, that's what I think too. And yet it seems that Carise, you and I are all mistaken: I'm not beautiful, I'm ugly.
MESRIN:	Ugly? My Adine ugly?
ADINE:	Yes, your own Adine. When I left you, Mesrin, I came upon a person from another world. And this person wasn't astonished by my presence as you are, she wasn't enraptured; no, this person demanded of me that I be delighted by her. And when I refused, she accused me of being ugly.
MESRIN:	What an outrage!
ADINE:	And she said you would leave me the moment you set eyes on her.
CARISE:	That's because she was vexed with you, Adine.
MESRIN:	Are you absolutely certain this was a real person?
ADINE:	She said she was and she looked like a person – more or less.

CARISE:	She is a person.
ADINE:	She may come this way and when you see her I want you to scorn her. I want you to be horrified by her.
MESRIN:	She must be revolting.
ADINE:	She's called . . . wait, what is she called. . .
CARISE:	Eglé.
ADINE:	Ah yes, she's an Eglé. You'll know her by an angry, scowling face, which isn't as dark as Carise's but isn't as white as mine. It's just a colour, a nondescript colour.
MESRIN:	Which isn't attractive.
ADINE:	Oh, no, not at all. Indeed it can hardly be called a colour at all. And her eyes. How can I describe her eyes? They are eyes that look, that's all. Her mouth is neither very large nor very small, it's a mouth to speak with. Her figure's upright and it would be similar to ours if only it were more pleasant to look at. She has hands that move about, and long, thin fingers. And her voice is rough and cross. You'll recognise her as soon as you see her.
MESRIN:	Look, I see a person over there, coming this way. Leave it to me: I'll send her back to her world thoroughly humbled.
ADINE:	Yes. Humiliate her, Mortify her.
MESRIN:	Don't worry. And now please let me have your hand.
ADINE:	Take it, Mesrin, it's here for you.
CARISE:	You've said all you wanted to say, Adine, let's go.
ADINE:	Only when he's finished kissing my hand.
CARISE:	Leave her alone, Mesrin, I'm in a hurry.
ADINE:	Goodbye, my love, I'll come back soon. Don't forget to avenge me.
MESRIN:	How can I fail when I am so angry with this person? Goodbye, my enchantress.

SCENE THIRTEEN

Mesrin, Azor.

MESRIN: A colour that's neither black nor white. An upright figure. A mouth that speaks. Where shall I find her? *(Seeing Azor.)* Is that her over there? Is that Eglé? No, I don't think it càn be. That person isn't deformed.

AZOR: Hello. You seem to be very similar to me.

MESRIN: That's what I was thinking.

AZOR: Are you a man then?

MESRIN: So I've been told.

AZOR: That's what I've been told as well.

MESRIN: You say you've been told: do you know some other people?

AZOR: Yes, I know all the people in this world. Two are black and one is white.

MESRIN: It's the same for me. Where are you from?

AZOR: The world.

MESRIN: Do you mean my world?

AZOR: I don't know. There seem to be so many worlds suddenly.

MESRIN: It doesn't matter anyway. I like your face. Put your hand in mine, we must love each other.

AZOR: You make me feel merry, and I like to look at you, although you're not exactly lovely.

MESRIN: Nor are you. What I like about you is that you're a man.

AZOR: That's it. That's my feeling for you. You're a good companion, I'm a good companion and I don't care about your looks.

MESRIN: Looking at you brings me good cheer. When do you take your meals?

AZOR: Every day.

MESRIN: So do I. Let's take our meals together, for our amusement and to keep us merry. We'll laugh, we'll jump about, isn't that right? I'm in such good spirits I'm already jumping.

He jumps.

AZOR: I'm jumping as well. There will be the two of us, there might even be three of us: I'll tell my pale beauty about this. Now, she does have looks I care about. Wait until you see her: she's worth more than the two of us put together.

MESRIN: I can believe that, my friend, because you and I are absolutely nothing next to someone I know, and who'll soon join us. She's a delight, and she has these soft white hands and she allows me to kiss them.

AZOR: Hands, eh? Well my pale beauty also has hands which are heavenly and she allows me to caress them as much as I want to. I'm expecting them right now.

MESRIN: Good, because I've just left the hands that belong to me and that reminds me I must leave you to attend to a little affair. Stay here until I come back with my dear Adine and let's jump some more to celebrate this happy meeting. Hahaha. Jump.

AZOR: Hahahaha. I'm jumping.

SCENE FOURTEEN

Azor, Mesrin, Eglé.

MESRIN: Look, look over there. There's a beautiful object which is listening to us.

EGLE: There's something standing next to Azor which looks most pleasing.

AZOR: That's my pale beauty, my Eglé.

MESRIN: *(To himself.)* Eglé? Adine calls that a scowling face?

AZOR: Ah, Eglé, I'm so happy.

EGLE: Is this a new friend who has suddenly appeared to us?

AZOR: Yes, he's a companion of mine. He's called a man and he comes from a world not far from here.

MESRIN: But this world is the best world.

EGLE: Why? Is there more to see here than in your world?

MESRIN: Oh yes, much more.

EGLE: Why then, you must stay here.

AZOR: That's just what we were saying. He's good and full of cheer and I love him. Not in the way I love you, my lovely Eglé, because I adore my Eglé, whereas I'm not too bothered about him. But I love to be in his company and to speak to him about you, about your mouth, about your eyes, about your hands. Ah, your hands, I've been languishing for your hands. Let me kiss them.

MESRIN: You kiss that hand, Azor and I'll kiss the other one.

EGLE: Ah.

AZOR: No. Wait. I want the other hand as well. This isn't your pale beauty, it's mine and both of these hands belong to me. There's nothing for you here.

EGLE: He wasn't doing any harm, Azor. By the way, it's time for you to go now. Remember how necessary separations are to our love. Yours hasn't lasted long enough.

AZOR: But I haven't seen you for hours!

EGLE: You're wrong. I know it hasn't been long enough. I'm determined to keep to what we've resolved.

AZOR: You'll be here all by yourself.

EGLE: I'll manage.

MESRIN: Don't upset her, friend.

AZOR: Are you angry with me, Eglé?

EGLE: Why are you being so stubborn? Weren't you told how dangerous it was for us to see too much of each other?

AZOR: It may not be true.

EGLE: I'm certain it wasn't a lie.

AZOR: I'll leave then, for your sake, but I'll be back soon. Come, my friend, you said you had some business to attend to. Come with me and help me pass the time.

MESRIN: Yes . . . but . . .

EGLE: What is it, friend?

MESRIN: I've been walking for such a long time.

EGLE: Then your friend must stay here and rest, Azor.

MESRIN: Yes, and I'll keep the beautiful woman company. That way she won't feel bored.

AZOR: She said she wanted to be alone, friend. If she needs to be entertained, I can do it much better than you. Let's go.

EGLE: *(Angry, aside.)* Go then.

SCENE FIFTEEN

Carise, Eglé.

CARISE: You seem very thoughtful, Eglé.

EGLE: Yes. I'm thoughtful about the fact that I'm in a bad mood.

CARISE: Are you feeling sad?

EGLE: No, Carise, it's not sadness, it's a kind of confusion.

CARISE: About what?

EGLE: You said before one never knew what might happen to love.

CARISE: Yes.

EGLE: Well, I don't know what's happening to me.

CARISE: What's wrong with you?

EGLE: It seems to me I'm angry with myself, I'm angry with Azor, I'm angry with everybody.

CARISE: Why are you angry with yourself?

EGLE: Because although I have the intention of loving Azor forever, I'm beginning to fear I might fail.

CARISE: Is that possible?

EGLE: Yes. I'm very cross with Azor and I suspect his behaviour is at fault.

CARISE: I think it may be that you want to find fault with him.

EGLE: If you keep answering me in that manner, I'll soon be angry with you as well.

CARISE: You are indeed in a bad mood. What has Azor done to you?

EGLE: Azor and I agreed to separate. He left but then he came back almost as soon as he'd gone. He wants to be with me all the time and what you predicted has begun to happen already.

CARISE: What? Could you suddenly love him less?

EGLE: Yes. It's not my fault if the pleasure one takes in seeing someone vanishes when one sees them too often.

CARISE: But you said that was impossible.

EGLE: Don't quibble with me. What did I know? I said that because I was so ignorant at the time.

CARISE: Eglé, I can't believe that it is Azor's desire to be with you all the time that's making you dislike him. You haven't known him long enough for that.

EGLE: Oh, I've known him long enough. We've already had three conversations together. Apparently, the length of these meetings has proved nefarious.

CARISE: You're not saying in what way you feel he has wronged you.

EGLE: He's wronged me in many ways. To begin with, he behaved with me in a most irritating manner. My hands are my own, I believe, I may do with them what I please, and he won't allow them to be kissed.

CARISE: And who wanted to kiss your hands?

EGLE: A friend Azor found recently and who's called a man.

CARISE: And you found this friend attractive?

EGLE: Yes, delightful. He has a more gentle manner than Azor and he was kind enough to offer to keep me company. Then Azor had the caprice of forbidding him the pleasure of my hand and me the pleasure of his company. He argued with his friend and then took him away. He never even asked what I wanted. Ha! Am I no longer my own mistress? Doesn't Azor trust me? Is he afraid someone else might love me?

CARISE: He may be afraid of your finding his friend too attractive.

EGLE: Then it's up to Azor to make himself a little more attractive to me. As for the rest, I like being loved by people and if Azor had a hundred friends instead of one, I'd want them all to love me. Azor wants my beauty to be there for him alone, but I think it should be there to be enjoyed by everybody.

CARISE: I believe your distaste for Azor isn't caused by
            that but by your present preference for Azor's friend.

EGLE: Do you think so? You could be right.

CARISE: Aren't you ashamed of your unfaithfulness?

EGLE: Yes, a little, but I'm still very ignorant about these
            matters.

CARISE: It's not ignorance, Eglé. You promised to love Azor
            and to remain faithful.

EGLE: Yes, but I promised that when he was the only one
            around. I didn't know about the existence of his friend
            then.

CARISE: You must admit those are not good reasons for being
            unfaithful and you denied them when Mesrou and I
            spoke to you before.

EGLE: You're right; they're not very good. I have one now
            that's irrefutable: It's simply that Azor's friend is better
            than Azor.

CARISE: You're wrong about that as well. It's not that he's
            better but that he's newer.

EGLE: Yes, but to be newer is a considerable advantage. It's
            an attractive quality and one that Azor completely
            lacks.

CARISE: Add to this that this newcomer is about to love you.

EGLE: Just so: I hope he is about to love me. That's another
            attraction.

CARISE: Whereas Azor is no longer about to love you.

EGLE: No, because he loves me already.

CARISE: You can't be very pleased with such peculiar reasons
            for your change of heart.

EGLE: I'm not pleased with anything. On the one hand, this
            change makes me sad, on the other, it makes me happy.
            I have no more control over the one than over the
            other. They are both equally important to me. Now, to
            which do I owe the most? Should I give myself pain or
            should I give myself pleasure? I challenge you to answer
            me.

CARISE: Consult your own heart: it'll condemn your
            unfaithfulness.

EGLE: You haven't been listening, Carise. My heart condemns
            it, but my heart also approves it. My heart says yes, my
            heart says no. It's of two minds. I suppose I might as
            well choose the most convenient.

CARISE: I'll tell you what to do. Avoid Azor's friend. That's the
            best way to resolve your struggle. Let's go quickly.

EGLE: I believe it's too late to go. The struggle is coming this
            way: Azor's friend is walking towards us.

CARISE: It doesn't matter. Make an effort, Eglé and don't look
            at him.

SCENE SIXTEEN

Mesrou, Mesrin,, Eglé, Carise.

MESROU: *(Trying to hold Mesrin back.)* Help me, Carise, he's running away from me. Don't let him come near: he wants to be unfaithful.

CARISE: Don't come any closer.

MESRIN: Why not?

CARISE: Because I forbid it. Mesrou and I must have some authority over you, we are your masters.

MESRIN: *(In revolt.)* Masters? You? I don't understand the notion of a master.

CARISE: Very well. If I can't order you not to come near, let me at least beg it of you. And Eglé will add her prayers to mine.

EGLE: Me? Not at all. I don't wish to add any prayers of mine.

CARISE: Let's go, Eglé. You don't even know if he loves you.

EGLE: I need only ask him. What do you want with me, handsome friend?

MESRIN: I want to see you, gaze upon your beauty, admire you and call you my dear soul.

EGLE: You see, Carise, he's even talking about his soul. And do you love me?

MESRIN: Desperately

EGLE: Didn't I tell you so, Carise?

MESRIN: Do you love me as well?

EGLE: I would prefer not to love you because there is Azor who loves me and is relying on me.

MESROU: Mesrin, follow Eglé's example and don't be unfaithful.

EGLE: Mesrin! So your name is Mesrin.

MESRIN: Yes.

EGLE: You're Adine's friend.

MESRIN: I was her friend but I don't even want her portrait any more.

EGLE: Give it to me. *(To herself.)* Adine's portrait and her friend. He has that merit as well. Carise, here are too many excellent qualities together and I can no longer resist them. Come here Mesrin, and let me love you.

MESRIN: What an enchanting hand, give it to me.

EGLE: I've gained an incomparable friend.

MESROU: Why do you want to leave Adine, Mesrin? What complaints do you have against her?

MESRIN: I'm not leaving Adine because I want to, but because Eglé's beautiful face commands it.

EGLE: He has eyes to see, that's all.

MESRIN: I know I am being unfaithful but there is nothing I can do about it.

EGLE: I've forced him to it, we've forced each other.

CARISE: Adine and Azor will be thrown into despair.

MESRIN: I'm sorry.

EGLE: What can we do?

CARISE: I could put an end to their unhappiness by making them love each other. Will you agree to that?

MESRIN: Yes, do it.

EGLE: No, wait. I want Azor to miss me, I feel my beauty deserves such a tribute. And it won't hurt Adine to suffer a little. It will teach her to know herself better.

SCENE SEVENTEEN

Mesrin, Eglé, Carise, Azor, Mesrou.

MESROU: I see Azor.

MESRIN: I now feel embarrassed before my friend. He'll be very surprised.

CARISE: It appears from the look on his face that he's already guessed the harm you've done him.

EGLE: Yes, he does look sad and he has a right to feel so.

AZOR: *(Approaches, shamefacedly.)* Eglé . . .

EGLE: Azor, are you upset?

AZOR: Yes.

EGLE: Very upset?

AZOR: Very.

EGLE: Yes, I see that you are. But how do you know that I love Mesrin?

AZOR: What?

MESRIN: Yes, my friend.

AZOR: Eglé loves you and no longer cares for me?

EGLE: Yes.

AZOR: *(Gaily)* Nothing could be better. Please go on loving each other. I no longer care for you either, Eglé. I'll be back in a moment, wait for me here.

EGLE: Stop. What do you mean, you no longer love me? What does that mean?

AZOR: I'll explain later.

SCENE EIGHTEEN

Mesrou, Carise, Eglé, Mesrin.

EGLE: Azor. Wait. Wait.

MESRIN: Don't call him back. You have no need for him now that you have me.

EGLE: Yes, but I would love you more if I could have him as well. I don't want to lose anything.

Carise and Mesrou laugh.

EGLE: I don't see what's so amusing.

SCENE NINETEEN

Mesrou, Carise, Eglé, Mesrin, Adine, Azor.

ADINE: *(Laughing)* There's the beautiful Eglé. If you ever want to see yourself again, you may come to me: I have your portrait. I obtained it without any difficulty.

EGLE: *(Throwing down Adine's portrait.)* Here's yours which I'm only too pleased to give back. It's not worth my keeping it.

ADINE: What? My portrait? Mesrin, what is she doing with my portrait?

MESRIN: I gave it to her.

EGLE: Azor, I wish to speak to you for a moment.

MESRIN: Why do you want to speak to him, Eglé? What about me?

ADINE: Come here, Mesrin, you seem to have taken leave of your senses.

SCENE TWENTY

*Mesrou, Carise, Eglé, Mesrin, The Prince, Hermiane, Adine, Meslis,
Dina, Azor.*

HERMIANE: No. Stop this. Stop this outrage. I refuse to see any
more, your Highness. I find Adine and Eglé
intolerable. Why did you choose women who would
display the most contemptible aspects of my sex?

EGLE: Who are all these people, Carise? They look very angry.
I want to go away.

They all start to go.

CARISE: Stay here, all of you, and don't be frightened. These
are all new friends and we must hear what they think.
Ah, Dina, Meslis, you're here too. Good.

MESLIS: Hello, Carise. Look at all these new people, Dina.

DINA: Yes, but we have no need of them, do we?

MESLIS: No, we don't. There isn't a person here who can
compare with you. Are these men or women, Carise?

CARISE: Both. The women are over there, and the men here.
Look at the women, Meslis and if you see one who
appeals to you more than Dina does, we'll give her to
you.

EGLE: I could accept your friendship. What is your name?

MESLIS: My name is Meslis, but I have no friendship to offer
you.

CARISE: Choose another woman, Meslis.

MESLIS: Thank you, Carise. They are all lovely but none of
them interests me. There is only one Dina in this
world.

DINA: That was beautifully said, Meslis.

CARISE: And you Dina, why don't you look at the men?

DINA: I've seen all there is to see. Let's go, Meslis.

HERMIANE: What an enchanting child. Let me look after her, your
Highness.

THE PRINCE: Do. And I'll take care of Meslis.

DINA: We don't need anyone else. We only want to be together.

THE PRINCE: Have no fears, we won't separate you. Carise, set Dina and Meslis apart and I will decide what to do with the others. Hermiane, I'm afraid neither sex has grounds to condemn the other. Vices and virtues seem to have been equally distributed amongst them.

HERMIANE: No, your Highness, you must allow for a difference. The treachery of your sex is revolting. Men change for no reason at all and don't even try to excuse their behaviour.

THE PRINCE: I admit that the conduct of your sex is more hypocritical and as such more decent. Women make a greater fuss over their conscience.

HERMIANE: Believe me, your Highness, this is no laughing matter. Let's go.

THE PRINCE: Yes, let us all go back to the court, and try once again to resolve this dispute.

THE END